# MOUNT VERNON
## The Story of a Shrine

The Story of the Rescue and Continuing
Restoration of George Washington's Home

BY GERALD W. JOHNSON

EPILOGUE BY
ELLEN MCCALLISTER CLARK

*Extracts from the Letters and Diaries of
George Washington*

SELECTED AND ANNOTATED BY
CHARLES CECIL WALL

*Published Through the Generosity of
The William Randolph Hearst Foundation*

THE MOUNT VERNON LADIES' ASSOCIATION
MOUNT VERNON, VIRGINIA
2002

*Library of Congress Cataloging-in-Publication Data*

*Johnson, Gerald W. (Gerald White), 1890-1980.*
*Mount Vernon: The Story of a Shrine: the story of the rescue and*
*continuing restoration of George Washington's home by the*
*Mount Vernon Ladies' Association/Gerald W. Johnson;*
*epilogue by Ellen McCallister Clark.*
*p. cm.*
*"Extracts from the letters and diaries of George Washington,*
*selected and annotated by Charles Cecil Wall."*
*Reprint, with new introduction, epilogue, and illustrations.*
*Originally published: New York: Random House, 1953.*
*Includes index.*
*ISBN-0-931917 17-4*
*1. Mount Vernon (Va.: state) 2. Mount Vernon Ladies' Association of*
*the Union—History. I. Washington, George, 1732-1799. II. Wall,*
*Charles Cecil (1903-1995). III. Clark, Ellen McCallister, 1953-. IV.*
*Title.*
*E312.5. J6 1991*
*975.5'291—dc20                    91-16151*
*CIP*

*Cover photograph by Robert C. Lautman*

# MOUNT VERNON

*The Story of a Shrine*

# INTRODUCTION

he history of historic preservation in America begins with Mount Vernon. In 1853, Ann Pamela Cunningham took up the cause of saving and restoring the home of George Washington, a place already identified in the hearts of Americans as a national shrine. While her vision sparked the first national historic preservation movement, her organization, the Mount Vernon Ladies' Association of the Union, also lays claim to being the oldest national women's society. Formed at a time when women had little role in public affairs, the Association's example of effective organization furthered the cause of women's rights.

The early success of the Mount Vernon Ladies' Association is all the more remarkable because its members came together from nearly every state at a time when the nation was bitterly divided, and held fast to their goal as the Union was wrenched apart by the Civil War. They were finding their way in a yet-to-be-defined field, with limited resources and primitive methods, and yet they launched a standard of preservation that would be the model for countless other historic places. Each succeeding generation of Mount Vernon ladies has found inspiration in the courage and wisdom of our predecessors, as we face the challenges and opportunities of our own times to carry forward their important work.

To mark our centennial in 1953 the Association sponsored the publication of *Mount Vernon: The Story of a Shrine*, an account of

*All Vice Regents of the Mount Vernon Ladies' Association wear this badge during Council meetings and other Association activities.*

I

our first hundred years as keepers of Washington's beloved home.

The author, Gerald W. Johnson (1890–1980), is today still recognized as one of the most prominent American journalists and essayists of the 20th century, ranking with Walter Lippmann and H. L. Mencken, of whom he was a protege. In the course of his long career, which included nearly two decades as an editorial writer for the Baltimore *Sunpapers* and 26 years as a contributing editor of *The New Republic*, he wrote more than 30 books of history, biography and commentary on American politics and culture. A progressive Southerner and stern social critic, he was also a patriot and optimist who saw in Mount Vernon's story a truly American tale of the triumph of popular initiative, made doubly significant by the fact that it was carried through by women. In his distinctive literary style, Johnson presented the real drama of the Association's struggle to save Mount Vernon and the ongoing quest to, in the words of Ann Pamela Cunningham, "keep it the home of Washington." This is the behind-the-scenes story of America's most important secular shrine, a place that has inspired and renewed the faith of millions and millions of her citizens over the generations.

This new edition of *Mount Vernon: The Story of a Shrine* republishes Gerald W. Johnson's text as it originally appeared, with a few new footnotes to put some passages in modern context. We have added an epilogue, written by Mount Vernon's former Librarian, Ellen McCallister Clark, that continues the story from 1953 to the present, highlighting the major achievements and events of the past 38 years. While the march of time has brought extraordinary changes, there is a remarkable continuity of purpose in our work that links us to the past.

As in the original edition our book concludes with a selection of extracts from the diaries and letters of George Washington annotated by Charles C. Wall, now Mount Vernon's Resident Director Emeritus. Mr. Wall, who has studied George Washington and Mount Vernon for more than 60 years, knows the subject as does no other scholar. These passages from Washington's writings bring to life the man as architect, farmer, husband and neighbor; the creator of Mount Vernon. In Washington's passion for order and beauty and his meticulous attention to every detail one can see reflected the true greatness of his character. It is this unmatched written record that has been the foundation of our work, allowing us to come ever closer, in physical detail and in spirit, to Mount Vernon as Washington knew it.

Around the time of the Association's centennial, the Regent noted in her annual address to Council that "nothing at Mount Vernon is ever complete." This was not a statement of frustration, but instead evidence of a true understanding of the nature of historic preservation. To accept Miss Cunningham's challenge to keep Mount Vernon the home of Washington requires constant and diligent work, calling upon the best resources of our age. Recently, the Association completed an intensive long-range planning and resources study covering every aspect of the Mount Vernon operation. While methods and perspectives change with the times, it is reassuring to realize that our ultimate mission remains straightforward and constant as we move toward future endeavors.

This new edition is dedicated to Ann Pamela Cunningham and the Vice Regents of the Mount Vernon Ladies' Association, past and present, whose stories are told within its pages. Our deep gratitude goes to the William Randolph Hearst Foundation which, among many generous contributions to Mount Vernon, provided the funds for the new edition of this enduring chronicle of our history.

*Eugenia Merrill Seamans*
*Regent, 1986–1990*

# I. INCEPTION

dmiral Sir George Cockburn, sometime of his Britannic Majesty's Navy, is remembered by Americans, but not with affection, although he once did them a favor. Admiral Cockburn (pronounced, incomprehensibly, "Co-burn"), was the officer commanding the naval squadron that raided and burned the city of Washington during the War of 1812, for which he is remembered without enthusiasm.

But as he dropped down the Potomac River after the raid, and his flagship, the *Sea Horse*, came opposite Mount Vernon, where George Washington had died 15 years earlier, he ordered the ship's bell tolled as she passed. It may be that Sir George was of a sardonic temperament, and this was a last defiant gesture on his part; or it may be that he was a genuine admirer of the most eminent of Americans. The latter explanation is not impossible, for in the early 19th century it was by no means unthinkable for a fighting man to hold, and express, high respect for an honorable foe.

In any event, that was the interpretation put upon it when the story got around, and the American boatmen on the river were somewhat abashed to find themselves outdone in politeness by a British naval officer; so thenceforth it was an established tradition of the Potomac that every craft equipped with a bell must toll it in

*The Mansion at Mount Vernon sits high on a bluff overlooking the Potomac River, opposite from the Maryland shore.*

passing Mount Vernon. This is, at least, one account of the origin of the custom, although proud patriots are slow to accept it.

The tradition was still strong 40 years later, and it was the tolling of a Potomac steamboat's bell that aroused the attention of a woman passenger one night in 1853. It happened that the moon was full and the right bank of the river was flooded with light, revealing details almost as plainly as they could be seen by day. It was not an inspiring sight that the old Mansion presented. The paint was peeling from the walls, the roof was sagging, at least one of the great pillars along the front had collapsed and been replaced by scantlings, the lawn was waist-high in rioting weeds. It was a picture of neglect, decay, and desolation, and the passenger could not get it out of her mind. The more she thought of it, the more bitter she became and the more ashamed of the way the country was permitting the home and burial place of its greatest hero to go to ruin.

The next day she wrote to her daughter, describing the scene and her emotions on viewing it. She ended with a question that had crossed her mind. If the men composing the Congress of the United States and the Legislature of Virginia, both of which bodies had been approached but had refused to act, were so careless of the great past, why should not the women of the South get together and save this relic?

That letter set off the chain reaction that rescued Mount Vernon. To cut a very long story down to its bare bones, the daughter organized and incorporated an association composed of a woman from each of the United States, that association raised $200,000 and bought the place, raised more money and reconditioned it, and has since held it inviolate for a hundred years.

Today, over one million people a year visit Mount Vernon, making it by far the most important place of secular pilgrimage in the country. Jamestown, Plymouth, Independence Hall, the bridge at Concord, and the field at Gettysburg, are all national shrines, but none makes the appeal to the American mind that is made by the home and tomb of George Washington.

*By 1858, when the Mount Vernon Ladies' Association purchased the estate, the Mansion was in a shocking state of disrepair.*

The overwhelming majority of the pilgrims are plain Americans, but the long procession is studded with glittering personages. The lords temporal and the lords spiritual of all the world have paid their tribute. An emperor and at least five kings, some before and some after coronation, have bowed before the tomb, including three kings of England and the Princess who now reigns as England's Queen. The Archbishops of York and of Canterbury, Cardinals, including the one who is now Pope,* and leaders of Zionism have paid the respects of Protestant, Catholic, and Jew; nor have great Buddhist and Mohammedan leaders, when they visited this country, omitted a visit to Mount Vernon.

There is no other spot in the United States, not consecrated to the Deity, that is held in such reverence by all the American people;

*Pope Pius XII, who died in 1958.

7

and this makes it shocking, in the eyes of many, that the place is not the property of the United States government, but of a few dozen individuals, not even officials of the government but private persons, legally on exactly the same status as the most obscure citizen who pays his admission fee at the entrance gate.

It is usually the case, however, that people who express this view have no acquaintance with the history of the organization or of the way in which it does its work. It can be argued plausibly that, far from being shocking, the legal status of Mount Vernon is very decidedly to the credit of the American people, and that the shrine is safer where it is than it would be were it transferred to official hands.

Mount Vernon as it stands today is the home of Washington. It is not a museum of American history, it is not a monument to the Revolution, it is not a public hall for patriotic meetings, and most emphatically it is not a showplace exploited for private profit. The only people who have every drawn a dollar from Mount Vernon are the workmen who keep the place in repair, the guards who protect it, their supervising officials, and certain technical experts, including the superintendent of the estate.

The Mount Vernon Ladies' Association of the Union holds the legal title to the property. This Association consists, in theory, of a Regent, who is the presiding officer, and one Vice Regent from each state. As a matter of practical fact the complement of Vice Regents is never full, so it is inexact to say that Mount Vernon belongs to 48 women;* the number is smaller.

The Regent and Vice Regents are unpaid. On the contrary, membership in the Association is almost sure to cost the member money, and quite sure to cost her time and thought and energy. The only compensation of the Vice Regent is the privilege of remaining on the place after the gates have been closed to the general public and of entering before they are opened. At some distance from the Mansion, but still on the grounds, is a guesthouse for the accommodation of members during their visits.

*Or today, 50. Alaska and Hawaii joined the Union in 1959.

8

That is all. Yet a Vice Regency is, and has always been, a coveted distinction that many of the grandest *grandes dames* in America have struggled for in vain. Some of the members have possessed great wealth, some high social position, and some have been relatively poor and unknown to readers of the society columns; but all have been intelligent, and most of them have been successful leaders. The history of the Association for its first hundred years thus becomes a sort of epitome of the history of the intelligent American woman for the past century.

That history is startling in its changes. Not long ago when the Regent of the Association went to Mount Vernon in order personally to receive the President of the United States accompanied by George by the Grace of God of the United Kingdom of Great Britain and Ireland King, Defender of the Faith, Emperor of India,* nobody thought anything of it. The world would have been shocked if she had failed to go. Yet in 1853, when the woman who was to be the first Regent began the agitation that resulted in the salvation of Mount Vernon, she was denounced for unladylike conduct in participating in public affairs. She herself was uncertain enough to sign a pen name to her first public manifestoes, for in her circle it was agreed that a lady's name could appear in the newspapers on two occasions only, her marriage and her funeral.

These instances, although they may appear to be, and in fact may be, trivial, by their contrast reveal a revolution in manners and customs that is far indeed from trivial. It is a revolution that has had more effect on the history of the United States than the campaigns of Grant, Shafter, Pershing, and Eisenhower combined; and that may in the end affect the history of the world as much as the elections of all the Presidents since 1853.

Every observer today knows that what America does affects not merely Georgia and Oregon, but Nepal and Peru as well; and what America is determines what America does. The status of its intelligent women is one of the most accurate measurements of what a na-

---

*HRH George VI and Queen Elizabeth visited Mount Vernon on June 9, 1939.

*Resident Director Charles Cecil Wall (far left), and Mrs. Horace Mann Towner, Regent (fourth from left) escort King George VI and Queen Elizabeth of England during the royal visit of 1939. Eleanor Roosevelt can be seen behind Mrs. Towner.*

tion is, so the story of this typical group for the past hundred years is more than an account of a particular enterprise. It is also a revelation of the social and moral development of one of the two most formidable powers on earth.

The story falls naturally into three divisions: Inception, Establishment and Refinement. They are not sharply marked off, but merge one into another with much overlapping; nevertheless, the first Regency, which lasted about 20 years, is clearly the period of Inception. Establishment is less clearly defined, but it certainly continued to the turn of the century, and it may be plausibly argued that it came down to the first World War. Refinement is still in process and may continue indefinitely. Each has its special interest not confined to Mount Vernon, but also as a strikingly faithful reflection of the social, as distinguished from the military and political, history of the United States. This is apart from the human interest attaching to any enterprise in which many persons with many divergent temperaments and points of view are involved, although that is great.

The opening chapter of the story is adorned by three admirable figures, two women and a man, a moral heroine, a physical heroine, and a patriot, each of whom was indispensable. Each of them came into the enterprise, the pious will say providentially, the cynical will say accidentally, anybody will say inadvertently, meaning that they did not know what they were getting into; but if any one of them had failed the enterprise would almost certainly have collapsed. The three were Ann Pamela Cunningham, Sarah C. Tracy, and Edward Everett. As chance would have it, they represented the three important sections of the country in 1853, Miss Cunningham coming from a plantation in South Carolina; Miss Tracy from Troy, New York; Mr. Everett from Dorchester, Massachusetts. The Southerner started the thing, the New Englander popularized it, the New Yorker held it together through its first and greatest crisis. "Comparisons," quoth Dogberry, "are odorous," and none could be more so than an attempt to assess the relative importance of the contributions of these three. Each was altogether different from the other two, but each was essential. Let it go at that.

But of the trio there is no doubt that Ann Pamela Cunningham was far and away the most complex and interesting character. To begin with, she was a tragically frustrated personality. All accounts agree that she began life as a gay, lighthearted, extremely active child, the life of "Rosemont," her father's plantation in South Carolina. As she grew up, she became a horsewoman noted for her enthusiasm even in a day when everyone rode. Then, when she was 16, came calamity. She was thrown, and in the fall suffered an injury to her spine that baffled the local physician.

Her parents, Colonel and Mrs. Robert Cunningham, did all that was humanly possible for their only daughter. They were wealthy and spared no expense, but the injury was too much for the medical science of the day. Mrs. Cunningham took her daughter to the famous Dr. Hodge, in Philadelphia, but the best he could do for her was psychological rather than physical.

*Ann Pamela Cunningham by James Reid Lambdin, circa 1860.*

Prudery was so intense in those days that now no one knows exactly what happened to the poor girl because all accounts skirt around the injury with vague language. We know that it did not result in definite paralysis, that only part of the time was the victim "confined to her couch"—at the time no one would think of describing a lady as bedridden, because that would be indelicate. We know that it involved pretty continuous pain that frequently became severe enough to prostrate the sufferer, and that is about all.

If the writers of the time had been less bound by convention we might today form a much more just estimate of Ann Pamela Cunningham's courage. Medical science has made tremendous strides in the past hundred years, but even the most up-to-date practitioner confronted with a severe spinal injury knows that he is in for trouble, and plenty of it. Some injuries of that kind can produce hideous pain difficult to relieve even with all the armamentarium of the modern doctor, so there is no sound reason for assuming that this woman's real misfortune was simply in having lived too soon, on the theory that now her disability would easily be removed.

Hugh Lenox Hodge was, in fact, a great man, so if he could do little for the girl it is safe to say that no contemporary could have done more, and it is not beyond belief that his successors might have been equally unsuccessful.

One thing, though, Hodge did do for his patient—he strengthened her spirit. She continued to visit him for many years, invariably coming away calmed, cheered, and encouraged, and when he died, shortly before her own death, she lamented him as "my second father." Perhaps this is not strictly the practice of medicine, but it is a gift that many a modern physician may well envy.

Miss Cunningham had been a semi-invalid for 21 years when the incident occurred that was to give meaning and direction to her life. She was prepared for it in two ways, one of which has been emphasized even by her contemporaries, but the second of which has been ignored. In the first place, she had long realized that whatever activity might break the monotony of her days must be intellectual, not physical. Not for her were the dances, the hunting field, the theater-going, and the gadding about from plantation to plantation that comprised much of the social life of her time and circle. She, "confined to her couch" much of the time, could not even travel by the easiest conveyances available except with much difficulty and much suffering. Her mind was her only resource.

This was understood clearly by her friends, but then, and even 30 years later, writers professed astonishment that a Southern lady, nurtured in the way this one had been, had the daring to emerge from the sheltered life and participate openly in public affairs. They forgot, or chose to ignore, the fact that the very injury that had made her a prisoner in most ways had in one way been a release. It had lifted from her the suspicion of personal ambition. In view of her physical condition such a charge against Ann Pamela Cunningham would have been preposterous, and she knew it—sadly, perhaps, but definitely. She could, therefore, cross with impunity the boundaries—the extremely narrow boundaries—of convention that hedged in all others and that they dared not breach.

Even so, when the letter from her mother fired her imagination the hold of tradition upon her was too strong to permit her to step out into the open at once. The suggestion that the women of the South should take upon themselves the labor of restoring and caring for the home of Washington obsessed her mind and became a terrific driving force. Obviously, the idea could not be realized until it was implanted in the minds of a great many other women, which involved a public appeal. Ann Pamela Cunningham was ready and willing and anxious to make it, but one thing gave her pause. The appeal could not be made anonymously—someone must stand behind it—but the prospect of having her name appear in the newspaper when she was neither married nor dead was at the start too much even for this bold spirit. Her first two or three communications she signed "A Southern Matron."

From the 20th-century standpoint this false modesty is amusing, but it was a deadly serious thing in 1853. When a few months later she did append her own signature to her appeals, there was much indignation among the old diehards, but by that time Ann Pamela

14

Cunningham was too much enthralled by the greatness of what she had started to be seriously disturbed by the criticism. It stung enough to make her resentful, but it did not appall her as it would have done a year earlier, and it did not give her a moment's pause.

The study of history would present no difficulty, or almost none, if it were possible for the present to recapture the style and spirit of the past. But that is precisely what we can never do, except partially and painfully. Of necessity we read a document of the 19th century with the eyes of the 20th century, but we also read it with the mental attitudes and the habits of speech of the 20th century, with the result that the effect of the document is distorted.

A case in point is the first public appeal of Ann Pamela Cunningham. It took the form of an open letter "To the Ladies of the South," dated December 2, 1853, and published in the Charleston *Mercury*. After a hundred years, however, the wording produces a completely false effect because the style of writing has changed. To modern taste it is flamboyant, affected, and pretentious. What we forget is that in 1853 such writing was regarded as good journalism. Miss Cunningham was not trying to produce a literary masterpiece; she was trying to produce an effect and she sensibly adopted the means most likely to produce it.

Today a manifesto filled with references to vestal virgins, altar fires, shades of the dead, worldlings, vultures, souls aflame, and Southern honor would amaze more readers than it would inspire; but in 1853 that was the ordinary style of oratory and newspaper writing. Therefore, in 1853 they took all that for granted and were the more easily able to perceive what we, entangled in the unaccustomed grandiloquence, are prone to overlook, namely, the intense earnestness of this appeal. The woman meant every word she said; and after a hundred years there is at least one paragraph that has been borne out to the letter. It reads:

*A spontaneous work like this would be such a monument of love and patriotism as has never been reared to patriot or mortal man; and while it would save American honor from a blot in the eyes of a gazing world, it would furnish a shrine where at least the mothers of the land and their innocent children might make their offering in the cause of the greatness, goodness, and prosperity of their country!*

That much has come to pass. During the century since those words were written Mount Vernon has received many rich gifts from the wealthy and distinguished; but the ordinary, daily labor of keeping the place in condition is paid for, not by the contributions of millionaires, but by the coins paid at the gate by the multitudes that visit the place. It has been in the most literal sense a classless enterprise.

The proof of the pudding is the eating thereof. Whatever we may think of the literary style of "A Southern Matron," her appeal was successful. The letter was copied by newspapers all over the South, and presently some in the North picked it up. "A Southern Matron" had suggested that contributions be sent to the governor of the contributor's state, to be by him transmitted to the governor of Virginia, who should effect the purchase.

But these gentlemen, who had not been consulted, apparently viewed the proceedings with a marked lack of ardor. It soon became clear that no such procedure would work, so, after a few more impassioned appeals, Ann Pamela Cunningham came out from behind the disguise of "A Southern Matron," organized a committee, and began to receive contributions in her own name; which brings the play down to the entrances of the second of the three star players, the Patriot.

The Reverend and Honorable Edward Everett, Ph.D., Phi Beta Kappa, Member of Congress, Governor of Massachusetts, Minister to Great Britain, United States Senator, President of Harvard, pastor of various churches, and greatest of the Silver Tongues of his generation, is one of the victims of history in a sardonic mood. His was the singular destiny to rise magnificently to the greatest opportunity of his whole career, only then and there to be squashed by inadvertence.

In 1863 his reputation as an orator was far and away above that of any other American speaker, so when the time came to dedicate the bloodiest and most important battlefield of the Civil War, there was no question that Everett was the man to make the principal speech. He realized fully the importance of the occasion, and the oration he delivered was very nearly, if not quite, the best he ever made. But when he sat down, the President was asked, by way of a brief epilogue before dismissal of the crowd, to say a few words. He did just that—he rose and said a few words. But those few words were Lincoln's Gettysburg Address, and if the whole mass of the hill called Round Top had fallen upon poor Everett he would not have been more completely obliterated. Lincoln did not intend anything of the kind. It was entirely inadvertent on his part, but it exposed with cruel clarity the difference between brilliance and greatness and the incident has had the effect of obscuring much of Everett's admirable quality.

For the mighty Lincoln himself was not a more ardent patriot than Edward Everett. Every act of his career proves it, and none more clearly than his course in the days when the great quarrel over slavery was building up and Everett was not sure enough of his own righteousness and wisdom to be willing to shatter the union rather than yield a jot of his opinion. This brought down upon him fierce denunciation from the fanatics, but it looks better after a hundred years.

One of this man's most important services to the country was his application of the thoroughness of German scholarship—he had taken his doctor's degree, the first ever given an American, at Gvttingen—to the study of American history. A by-product of this study was a lecture, prepared for delivery in Boston, on George Washington as a builder of the Union; it was so successful that he was asked to repeat it in Richmond, Virginia, and there in 1856 he encountered Ann Pamela Cunningham, who told him what she was trying to do with regard to Mount Vernon.

At this time, Mount Vernon, after a curiously zigzag descent, was owned by John Augustine Washington, Jr., who found it a white elephant. To start with, more than a hundred years before the outbreak of the Revolution—in 1674, to be exact—Lord Culpeper, who held from the King, granted 5000 acres, including this property, to two purchasers, Nicholas Spencer and John Washington. In 1690 the tract was divided between the Spencer heirs and the Washington heirs, the part that is now known as Mount Vernon going to John Washington's son, Lawrence, who left it to his daughter, Mildred, who sold it to her brother Augustine, who built the original house and later deeded it to his son, Lawrence. Lawrence left a life tenure to his widow who leased the property to her brother-in-law, George, the residuary heir, who added to the house and left it as we see it now to his nephew, Bushrod, a Justice of the Supreme Court, who left it to his nephew, the first John Augustine, who left it to his wife, Jane C., who left it to her son, the second John A., in whose hands it was at mid-century.

But from Bushrod down the line to John Augustine, Jr.—and it may be that one could also say, up the line to the original John—there was not a farmer worthy to be named in the same breath with George, who was almost, perhaps quite, as great in agriculture as he was in statecraft. In the hands of owners not endowed with his genius the Mount Vernon estate followed the course of most Virginia farm property, steadily losing its fertility and steadily becoming less profitable.

John Augustine, Jr., not only saw his income from the property dwindling year by year, but was also subjected to a unique financial drain by his mere occupancy of what had already become a national shrine. Throngs of people came to see the home of George Washington and John Augustine felt bound by the code of a Virginia gentlemen to receive them hospitably. The result was that eventu-

*The great orator and statesman Edward Everett single-handedly raised almost $70,000 in the 1850s to help the Association purchase Mount Vernon.*

*John Augustine Washington, Jr., great-grandnephew of George Washington and the last private owner of Mount Vernon.*

ally he found himself in such financial straits that he could not maintain the property in good condition. This harsh necessity, and not any stolid indifference to the historical significance of the place, accounts for the fact that he allowed it to fall almost into ruin.

He revealed that he had been approached by speculators who offered him $300,000 for the property, intending to commercialize it. To this he could not consent, but his obligations were becoming intolerable, so he approached Congress, offering Mount Vernon, including the Mansion and some 200 acres surrounding it, to the nation for $200,000. But Congress was not interested. In fact, some ingenious member dug up a legal opinion to the effect that the United States could not buy a foot of land within any State from an individual, but only from the State itself. Washington accordingly approached the Virginia Legislature, offering the same terms. But the Legislature seems to have been suspicious. It could not visualize letting the State in for an expenditure of $200,000 with no assurance that Congress would take the property off its hands; and no one familiar with the record of Congress in financial matters can blame it much. In any event, Washington got nowhere, and became a decidedly soured man. So when Ann Pamela Cunningham began to talk of purchase by the ladies' association, he merely grunted. He didn't say yes and he didn't say no.

But the optimistic Miss Cunningham, since he had not definitely refused, seems to have assured Everett that it was merely a matter of raising $200,000. This was matter enough, in all conscience, for the dollar was worth at a conservative estimate at least three times what it is now. The modern reader should think of not less than $600,000* to realize the magnitude of the job.

However, the orator was a money-maker, which is another reminder of how times have changed. For our generation it is hard to believe that people gladly paid high admission prices to hear a man orate for two hours at a time; but in 1853—actually 1856, for three years had passed before Everett came to Richmond—successful lec-

*1953 dollars. The amount in today's money is perhaps incalculable.

21

turers were as opulent as popular television commentators are today. Everett was never a mercenary character—he gave away much of his earnings—but he did take in the cash, so the sum of $200,000 did not appall him.

He cheered, encouraged, and stimulated Ann Pamela Cunningham, but he did vastly more. He donated the proceeds of his Richmond lecture to the cause. Already he had been asked to repeat the lecture at Baltimore and other places, and he said he would thereafter donate the proceeds of that lecture wherever he delivered it. To cut a long story short, within the next three years he lectured on Washington 129 times, in every part of the country, and at every lecture he publicized what the Mount Vernon Association was trying to do, which resulted in contributions.

Soon he had a considerable sum in his hands, so he appointed three of his friends, shrewd Boston businessmen, as trustees to hold the money. They invested it, promptly and smartly, so it began to increase by interest. Then a New York newspaper, the *Ledger*, made a proposal to Everett for a weekly article on some phase of American history. He agreed to do 52—a one-year contract—provided the *Ledger* would pay into the Mount Vernon fund, in advance, the sum of $10,000. It was done, and that too was invested; so for a year Everett turned out an article running between two and three columns every week, without putting a cent into his own pocket.

In the end, what with the lectures, the newspaper articles, and the profit made by his trustees, he turned over to the Association $69,024, a little more than one-third of the whole price of Mount Vernon. A patriot indeed was the old Silver Tongue, a five-star patriot, a blue-ribbon patriot, who deserves far more credit from this generation than he has ever received.

So by 1858 Ann Pamela Cunningham was in a position to go to John Augustine Washington with the assurance that money in hand gives a negotiator.

Her financial position was no more sound than her legal status. Two other remarkable figures had seen to that. When the vague scheme of turning in money to various governors, they to remit to the governor of Virginia, had proved impractical, she had tried out two or three other ideas. One of her associates was related to John MacPherson Berrien—senator from Georgia, former attorney general, and eminent constitutional lawyer—who advised the creation of what we would now call a nonprofit corporation under the laws of Virginia. But the charter first granted looked suspicious to John Augustine Washington, who professed to see in it trick clauses that might be used to turn his property over to Virginia politicians for whom, by this time, he had no love whatever.

Berrien died in 1856, so Ann Pamela Cunningham turned, in this perplexity, to an odd character who had become a big lawyer in Charleston before she was born, James Louis Petigru. It was characteristic of her method never to fool with a second-rater. If she had need of a doctor, she went to Hodge, of Philadelphia. If she needed an orator, she picked Everett, of Boston. If she needed a lawyer, she consulted an ex-attorney general of the United States, and after his death, Petigru, of Charleston.

It was the kind of job to delight the old man because in the first place it was a patriotic service and, in the second place, it flew in the face of convention. For Petigru ranks with Everett as a patriot, and he deserved far more than the Duke of Alengon the title of The Malcontent. He had opposed the War of 1812, but joined the militia when it came. He had been a stubborn supporter of Andrew Jackson during the Nullification crisis, when Jackson's name was anathema in Charleston. A few years later he was to be an equally stubborn supporter of the Union right through the Civil War; when a stranger in Charleston asked the way to the insane asylum Petigru sardonically sent the man to the hall where the Secession Convention was sitting. Yet he was "arm'd so strong in honesty" that when he died in 1863, in the midst of war, his Confederate neighbors erected a monument with a glowing tribute to the Unionist.

This man happily took over Miss Cunningham's legal perplexities at a time when a majority of his colleagues at the bar regarded the incorporation of a group of females as definitely a crime against nature if not an act of absolute impiety. He drafted a completely new charter for her and it was invulnerable; it has since been attacked in the courts, in the Legislature of Virginia, and in the Congress of the United States, but it has withstood every assault.

Petigru changed even the name. Miss Cunningham had had it simply "The Mount Vernon Association," but Petigru's sense of justice rebelled at that. He inserted the word "Ladies" on the ground that the people who had done the work deserved the credit. As an Early Victorian gentleman of Charleston he was, of course, incapable of describing any reputable female as a "woman," so it had to be "ladies." With Bostonian Everett storming through the land, and contributions pouring in from Massachusetts and New York—and probably because of his own intense nationalism—he thought it prudent, also, to eliminate any possible taint of sectionalism from the enterprise and therefore put in "Union."

That is why for a hundred years the organization has been "Mount Vernon Ladies' Association of the Union." It is undeniably quaint. It is more than a little stiff. But it is also a bit stately and, above all, it is a true description. Quaint, stiff, stately, and true, it reflects old James Louis Petigru to the life, so, like his charter, it has stood for a century and nobody thinks of changing it now.

The amended charter was duly passed by the Legislature of Virginia, although not without some growling about a lot of pushing females thrusting themselves into business that had better be left to their lords and masters. So, with an unassailable legal status and with money in hand, Ann Pamela Cunningham at last was in position to go to John A. Washington to talk straightforward business, and to Mount Vernon she took her way.

Then on the very brink of success she almost came to grief. She found the proprietor in the worst of tempers, and she could not figure out why. From her point of view everything had been going along splendidly. She had not the entire purchase price in hand, but a very respectable part of it, and more money was coming in every day. She neither asked nor expected the owner to transfer title until the last dollar was paid, but she did expect that in consideration of a very substantial down payment he would enter into a contract for the sale.

But he was firm in his refusal. His ill-humor did not make Mr. Washington forget that he was a Virginia gentleman, receiving a lady in his home. His conduct was correct, but icily correct, and during a long evening all the arguments she could bring to bear he received in stony silence. At last, with cold civility, he left her and she went to bed in a state of collapse.

It was no wonder, for her spine had been giving her trouble and the long trip had been torturing. Then it was the month of April, and Mount Vernon is never more enchanting than in the spring. Its physical beauty had made her heart leap on her arrival, sure that this was what she was to secure for the nation; and the disappointment was all the more bitter for that.

What with everything, she spent a wretched night, falling into a troubled sleep not much before dawn—and then overslept. She was to return to Washington by boat, and when they got her down to the landing the boat had already pulled out and was in midstream. The jolting journey overland to Alexandria was out of the question, and there was nothing for it but to return to the house and wait for the next boat. Mrs. Washington was hospitality itself, so that did not greatly matter; the disappointment was the bitter thing.

So the visitor, rather halfheartedly by her own account, began to try to find out from the wife some explanation of her husband's attitude, and little by little it came out. In the course of the negotiations, and especially during the debate over the new charter, certain Virginia politicians had seen an opportunity to show their constituents what noble guardians of the public interest they were by tearing into Mr. Washington, and they had handled him roughly. Character assassination for political profit was assuredly no new thing, even in that day, but ordinarily the politicians knifed each other, not unoffending citizens such as Washington, who was not running for anything and had no intention to seek office. As far as he could see, it was a purely gratuitous assault.

He had said nothing, but every slanderous charge, every villainous insinuation, had rasped his very soul, for he had all the pride of a Virginia aristocrat whose honor had never been impugned before.

As his helpless fury mounted he began to hate the whole deal and everybody connected with it and eventually his hatred grew so overwhelming that it included even the innocent ladies of the Association. He came to suspect them of being parties to a conspiracy to brand him before the public as a conscienceless extortioner willing to trade upon his great name and the sacred memories attached to his house in order to thrust his covetous hands into the public treasury. The wonder is that he did not forget that he was a gentleman when an emissary of the Association appeared.

This was, however, something that Ann Pamela Cunningham could easily understand and her bewilderment vanished. More than that, if there was anything with which a South Carolinian was perfectly able to cope, it was a point of honor. Miss Cunningham was not a beautiful woman but she was decidedly a thoroughbred and all the world knows that when a well-bred woman of South Carolina deliberately sets herself to be a charming as she can possibly be, she is as nearly irresistible as is any type of humanity.

The art of diplomacy is poorer because there is no verbatim record of the conversation on that April morning when she went for John Augustine Washington full tilt, understanding at last what was really the matter. The outcome was what the judicious would predict as inevitable. It took some hours, but in such circumstances no Virginia gentleman would have a chance. So on April 6, 1858, Washington set his hand to a contract of sale to the Mount Vernon Ladies' Association of the Union.

The terms were $18,000 down, an additional $57,000 the following December, and the balance in four equal annual installments. As a matter of fact all, except about $6,000, was paid in less than three years.

Which brings the play down to the entrance of the third of the three stars.

Sarah C. Tracy, originally of Troy, New York, was not one of the

*During the Civil War, the Association's secretary Sarah Tracy lived in the Mansion and safeguarded the estate from danger.*

"Ladies" of the Mount Vernon Association. Indeed, as one examines the existing records that mention her, something keeps whispering that this attitude is familiar. When the Three Little Maids from School were presented to Pooh-Bah, his comment was, "They are not young ladies, they are young persons," and one cannot escape the suspicion that in the eyes of the Regent and Vice Regents, Sarah Tracy was not a young lady, she was a Young Person.

The trouble is that they were so very insistent that she *was* a lady. If there had been no doubt about it, why mention the point at all? Her birth and breeding were, it is true, impeccable, but she had to work for a living, and it is idle to deny that in 1853 a woman who worked for her living was presumably not a Lady but a Person; so when people found one who was also a Lady, they were astonished and made special mention of the fact. Even after Sarah Tracy had been proving her quality for years, Ann Pamela Cunningham, writing to a Vice Regent of "my secretary and friend" felt it necessary to add, "for she is a lovely woman." The implication that a great lady's friendship for a secretary called for explanation is an acid commentary on the times.

The records concerning Sarah Tracy are scanty. Indeed, nobody seems to have paid much attention to her astonishing contribution to the project until 1946, when Dorothy Troth Muir dug out of the original documents the remarkable story and published it under the title *Presence of a Lady*. But there is no possible doubt that she was one of the important contributors to the salvation of Mount Vernon.

She was brought to Ann Pamela Cunningham's attention in 1859, when the work of the Association was becoming so heavy that the Regent had to have secretarial assistance. But a confidential position of that sort was not to be filled carelessly, and the appointment was preceded by much anxious correspondence with all kinds of people. The final choice was made on a recommendation by Samuel Griswold Goodrich, almost unknown to fame as Goodrich, but well known indeed under his pen name of Peter Parley. He was in a way the Edgar Rice Burroughs of his time, but more prolific; where Burroughs turned out 50-odd books of the sort termed "juveniles" by the publishing trade, Peter Parley wrote—or at any rate signed—116. His tales, however, did not deal with an ape-man, but with American history, and they were regarded as edifying in the highest degree. Some of them were about as fictitious as *Tarzan*, but they did turn the minds of youngsters toward the record of the republic.

The incident is worth mention because it shows how the effort to save Mount Vernon had enlisted the interest of all kinds of people. The crippled aristocrat of Rosemont; the orator, scholar, and historian of Harvard; and a manufacturer of trumpery children's stories, were all keenly interested in an effort that seemed to command the admiration and support of every class—with one conspicuous exception. The gentlemen who controlled the appropriations in Congress and the legislature of Virginia were not interested. As individuals some of them may have contributed, but not one dollar of public money went into the Association treasury.

Perhaps this is not as strange as it seems. Remember that the period was the late 50s of the past century. Remember, too, that George Washington was the rock on which the Union was founded, and that in his Farewell Address to his countrymen he had earnestly warned them against developing a factional spirit that he feared would rip the Union apart. In the late 1850s factional spirit was doing exactly that, and politicians were leading the factions, daily urging on the fights, increasing the bitterness, inflaming the hatreds. In those circumstances it is easy to believe that they found mention of George Washington embarrassing and were little disposed to bring his memory vividly to mind. Oh, they constantly appealed to him, each in support of his own faction; but they wanted to use him, not to follow him, and it was not well to remind the country too clearly of a man whose work they were undoing. In any event, governmental agencies took no part in the rescue of Mount Vernon other than the action of the Virginia Legislature in granting a charter to the Association.

But the American people poured money into the treasury. Massachusetts sent $20,000 in addition to the tremendous contribution of Edward Everett, which was credited to Massachusetts although it

*Lithographs such as these 1858 views of the Mansion and tomb were sold by the Association to raise funds for the purchase of Mount Vernon.*

had been collected everywhere. New York sent more than $30,000, Alabama something over $10,000, California $9,500, Pennsylvania nearly $9,000, North Carolina $8,000 and so on. By the end of 1859 practically all the purchase money had been paid in, and John A. Washington agreed to turn over physical possession of the property even though formal title had not been transferred. To give the event a historically significant touch, it was suggested that he move out on Washington's birthday, February 22, 1860.

Long before that date Ann Pamela Cunningham had decided that as soon as the Washingtons moved out she would take up residence there so as to supervise personally the work of restoration, which was certain to be long and difficult. It had been begun, in fact, by consent of the Washingtons, several months earlier, under the superintendence of Upton H. Herbert, a Virginian with a personal interest in the work because his family was closely connected with the Washingtons.

Since the Superintendent was a Southerner, the Regent was pleased to have a secretary from New York, as giving the enterprise a more truly national look. As the Washingtons moved out, she and Sarah Tracy moved in.

At first, however, it would be more exact to say that they camped out at Mount Vernon, rather than resided there. The furniture, of course, belonged to the Washingtons, so very nearly all that the new occupants found in the place was the key of the Bastille, which Lafayette had given the General, the terrestrial globe in his study, and the original clay model of the Houdon bust, which Washington with his own hands had placed above the door of the study. Later, to protect it against damage and to exhibit it properly, it was placed in the museum. There were some kitchen utensils, but little else, so hasty trips to Washington had to be made for such necessities as beds and bedding as well as everything else.

Making the place livable took time, and it had hardly been accomplished when the increasing political uproar made it imperative for Miss Cunningham to return to South Carolina to look after her property there. It seems that at this time Miss Tracy had not even

31

been engaged on a permanent basis, but was merely serving until definite arrangements could be made. However, the Regent had no doubt that she could adjust her Southern affairs readily, so she expected to be gone only a few weeks, or at most a month or so. As it turned out, she did not see Mount Vernon again for more than six years. In December South Carolina seceded, and the Civil War was on, with Ann Pamela Cunningham trapped at her plantation home.

The United States Army promptly seized Alexandria, across the river from Washington, but it was only a bridgehead. The Potomac River was the line, and Mount Vernon was on the bank of the Potomac. The Federal lines were pushed down seven miles from Alexandria to within four miles of Mount Vernon. The Confederate lines were pushed up to about the same distance on the other side. In between was a no man's land in which cavalry patrols were constantly battling and across which the armies occasionally surged in heavier movements. As the war wore on something worse appeared than either cavalry patrols or columns of infantry in the shape of bushwhackers, claiming to be guerrilla fighters supporting now one side, now the other, but in reality little better than robber bands, capable of atrocious crimes. It was a situation of extreme peril.

There is no adequate picture of Sarah Tracy at Mount Vernon, only a small photograph, but contemporary accounts agree in portraying her as small, dainty, and modest, very pretty and probably very shy. Such was the young person suddenly plumped down between battling armies and responsible for the most precious historical shrine in America. The thunder of the guns of Bull Run rattled the windows of Mount Vernon, and a little later those of the second Bull Run; the collision at Aquia Creek was so close that rifle fire could be distinguished; late one evening the cavalry of the two

*Among the objects presented to the Association by departing owner John Augustine Washington, Jr., was the terra cotta bust of George Washington done from life at Mount Vernon in 1785 by Jean Antoine Houdon. The bust, one of the few objects that has never left Mount Vernon, is said to be the best likeness of Washington ever created.*

33

armies crashed together at a crossroads just south of the estate and battled all night long; and constantly stragglers, deserters, escaped prisoners, bushwhackers, all the flotsam and jetsam of a theater of war swarmed around the place.

Herbert, the Superintendent, stood by, apparently in a somewhat shamefaced manner. His brothers and all his friends were in the Confederate service, and over and over again he was offered a commission, but he had promised the Regent that he would take care of the place until her return, and he did. His usefulness, however, was limited to the estate. Had he once set foot in Alexandria he would have been arrested and compelled to take the test oath, which he was resolved not to do.

When Ann Pamela Cunningham left, while things were still relatively quite, Herbert's aunt had come from her nearby home to stay with Sarah Tracy until she could get someone else. But the aunt had her own family responsibilities, so when the Regent's return was delayed Sarah persuaded one of her friends to come, one whom we know only as a Miss McMakin, of Philadelphia.

For four long years, the four bloodiest and most desperate years in American history, the two ladies stuck it out. To the modern mind the whole idea seems fantastic to the verge of insanity; but the mind of the 20th century—we may as well face the fact—is more brutal than that of the 19th. The concept of total war is of our century; when they were fighting across the Potomac chivalry was not yet quite dead. Ann Pamela Cunningham was far indeed from being a cynic and, as the event proved, her idealism was well justified. When war was seen to be inevitable and the exposed position of Mount Vernon was realized, she advised Sarah Tracy to stay there, on the grounds that "the presence of a lady" would protect the place.

It did, and the fact that it did is eloquent of the change that a hundred years have wrought in the art of war. The American Civil War was an extremely violent one. The high proportion of casualties to the total number of troops engaged puts it among the most savage contests in human history, but by comparison with the collisions of the 20th century it was an astoundingly gentlemanly war. Commanders on both sides did not hesitate to sacrifice a military advantage rather than destroy a shrine of history, and the presence of a lady there made it unthinkable for them deliberately to open fire on the place.

But at that the perils were sufficiently appalling. When a battle is raging the knightliest commander cannot control the trajectory of a stray shot, and armies, as Kipling observed, are not composed of plaster saints. For four years Sarah Tracy had as close neighbors any number of villainous types. Perhaps an even greater danger was offered by the fact that the place was frequently encircled by green troops who knew they were very close to the enemy. A nervous sentinel on an extreme outpost is just about as dangerous to friend as to foe, having a strong tendency to shoot first and challenge afterward. On every trip to town Sarah Tracy had to pass a number of outposts, often after dark, and every such experience presented a chance of stopping a bullet meant for an enemy patrol.

Throughout the ordeal she wrote carefully-detailed reports to the Regent, as long as communication was possible, and to various Vice Regents thereafter. Many of her letters have survived, so we have a remarkably clear account of Mount Vernon during the Civil War. It is clear, that is to say, about every phase of the situation except one. There is not a word, never a hint, of the terrors that must have racked the soul of a shy young girl from Troy, New York, suddenly flung into the midst of the most frightful war her country had ever seen.

Perhaps from Ann Pamela Cunningham she had learned the advisability of always consulting the top man if possible. Immediately after the occupation of Alexandria Sarah made her way to Washington and somehow crashed the gate into General Headquarters. Winfield Scott was what we would now call Chief of the General Staff and she reached his office. To the adjutant, Major—later Colonel—Townsend she made the extraordinary demand of a pledge from the General that he would not fortify Mount Vernon, nor permit a single soldier under his command to enter the grounds under arms.

Townsend was certainly astonished and probably somewhat amused, but he was very courteous, and promptly took her request

into the General's private office. Presently he emerged and Sarah heard Scott say, "God bless the ladies!" before the door was closed. The adjutant, in Scott's name, promised everything she had asked, and gave her a pass through the Federal lines.

"But," he added soberly, "can you be as sure of Virginia?"

"Yes," said Sarah promptly, and that was that.

It is certainly the only time in history that the state of Virginia was committed to a military policy by a lady from New York, but the pledge was kept as faithfully as if it had been signed by the Governor and the whole Council of State. Yes, it was a gentlemanly war.

However, Sarah's troubles were only beginning. Herbert had assembled a crew of workmen, mostly Negroes, before the outbreak of war and as things tightened he made shift to feed them fairly adequately on produce grown on the estate. A handful of visitors still ventured out to Mount Vernon and paid admissions, which brought in a little cash. Sarah was away when one interesting party came down by boat from Washington—Mrs. Abraham Lincoln with a group of friends. She was there, though, one morning a year or so later when a group of gentlemen, apparently officers in mufti, came. She withdrew, leaving Herbert to show them about; for she records that while she did not mind conducting parties of enlisted men through the Mansion, she never took officers, because they were less polite—an interesting commentary on the social code.

However, when she thought they had all gone to visit the tomb she came down to prepare lemonade and, stepping into the dining room for a pitcher, found herself facing two of them. She bowed, they bowed. She made a remark about the heat of the day, and they looked puzzled. Then she remembered having heard earlier one member of the party say something in French, so she dug back in her mind for the schoolgirl French she had learned in New Orleans

*A sketch from the* New York Illustrated News, *December 16, 1861, depicting soldiers visiting Mount Vernon. The scene is the park slope between the Mansion and the river, with the icehouse vault entrance and the old summer house in the background.*

*As an artist-correspondent for* Harper's Magazine *in 1861, Winslow Homer was on his way to join the Army of the Potomac when he made this sketch of the Mansion.*

and tried it. They brightened immediately, and asked in French where to find a hotel, as they had left Washington early in the morning expecting to get breakfast on the way, but their guide had misled them and they had had nothing to eat. Sarah explained that there was no such thing as a hotel anywhere near, but offered them such a lunch as she could provide.

Obviously relieved, they overwhelmed her with thanks, and explained their embarrassment by informing her that they were staff officers of Prince Napoleon, who was then inspecting the tomb. So Sarah entertained the whole group and got along very well, since the Prince spoke excellent English. Finally, as their hired horses were exhausted, she sent them back to Alexandria behind a pair of the Mount Vernon mules.

Encounters with princes and generals, however, were rare highlights in a dark story of struggle against all sorts of difficulties. Again and again overzealous captains and lieutenants refused to honor Sarah's pass, and twice she actually ran the blockade, in which enterprise she might have been shot legitimately. It was necessary, for as money grew scarcer she had to sell produce from the farm in Washington in order to keep things going. Herbert couldn't go on pain of arrest; and although the authorities had at first given her a pass for a Negro teamster, all passes for servants were presently cancelled; so we have the spectacle, frequently repeated, of demure Miss Tracy, the fragile little girl from Troy, New York, driving a wagonload of cabbages to the Washington market, and coming back with meat, salt and pepper, and—on the rare occasions when they were to be had—coffee and tea. Fifteen miles is a long day's journey in a farm wagon behind a pair of mules. Even when she stayed in the city overnight, she was more than once overtaken by darkness before she got home, and then it was a question of watching for one of the many roadblocks set up against Confederate raiders, and hoping that the sentry on duty would not shoot first and inquire afterward, or that if he did shoot he would miss.

Again and again she had to detour around roadblocks by taking mere cart tracks through the woods and across fields. At least once she was halted altogether and had to spend the remainder of the night at an unknown farmhouse, and at least once—this time, fortunately, she was driving a buggy—friendly soldiers at a roadblock in thick woods, where it was impossible to drive around, led the mule through the thick brush, took the buggy apart and lifted it piece by piece over the roadblock, reassembled it, then lifted Sarah over, put her in the buggy and sent her on her way.

On September 13, 1861, John Augustine Washington, Jr., who had joined Lee's staff, was killed in an obscure skirmish in what is now West Virginia. Sometime later Sarah was informed that part of the money he had received for Mount Vernon he had left with a bank in Alexandria, and the Federal authorities were searching for it to seize it as enemy property. She was going into Washington with a basket of eggs for the market, so the money was turned over to her, wrapped in a paper parcel which she placed in the bottom of the basket and covered with eggs—but this story she never wrote in any of her letters and it rests on the authority of a citizen of Alexandria. Her pass was accepted that time, so she went to the bank of George W. Riggs, treasurer of the Association, and rented a safe-deposit box. Emptying the eggs on the banker's desk, while he watched without moving a muscle, she put the package in the box, locked it and pocketed the key. Then for the first time Mr. Riggs spoke.

"Hand me your purse," he said.

She did, and solemnly he tucked the egg money into it, handed it back with the empty basket, and she proceeded about her lawful occasions.

At last one day an outpost officer halted her and curtly informed her that General George B. McClellan had forbidden any pass to be honored, even one signed by General Scott, technically his superior.

A friendly farmer showed Sarah a woods path by which she ran the blockade again and gained Washington and General Scott's headquarters. The old man by this time was close to the end of his tether; drearily he informed her that if McClellan would not honor a pass signed by the Chief of Staff, there was nothing Scott could do about it. Nobody, in fact, could help Miss Tracy in the circumstances except, perhaps, the President of the United States.

So straight to the White House went the small, determined defender of Mount Vernon. What a loss to history it is that there is no transcript of that interview! All Sarah says is, "He received me very kindly and wrote a note to Mr. McClellan requesting him to see me and arrange the matter in the best way possible." McClellan denied that he had ever issued any such order, and immediately gave Miss Tracy a pass from his own headquarters.

But who cares what McClellan said or did? What would be worth any price to our generation is a picture of tall, angular Abraham Lincoln and this mite of a girl confronting each other. With what astonished amusement the ungainly giant must have looked down upon this bit of femininity who had burst in upon him bristling with indignation against his field commander, and demanding that he order the United States Army to stand aside while she passed with her groceries!

But trust a great man to recognize greatness of spirit wherever he encounters it. Undoubtedly Lincoln's lips twitched, but he did not laugh at Miss Tracy of Troy, because he knew she was doing her duty under great difficulty, and her duty was to the American Lincoln revered above all others. Perhaps this flash of loyalty and courage brightened his day; one at least may hope so.

This was Sarah C. Tracy, the lady whose presence protected Mount Vernon through four years of war, and none can deny that a lady of quality she was. Illness invaded the working crew, ague and fever, pneumonia, finally typhoid, and she perforce became doctor—she wrote "Doctress"—and nurse. When a party of soldiers came, merely as visitors, not under arms, Herbert found a young lieutenant lying under a tree in delirium; it appeared that he was just out of the hospital after a bout of "congestive fever," whatever that was. His comrades had sent for an ambulance, but he was too sick to be moved and Sarah had him put to bed in the house and nursed him for four days, at what risk of infection she did not know, nor anyone else.

Diet on the place was supplemented by fish from the Potomac and fishing from the boat pier in the early morning became part of the family routine, everyone participating. One morning when the two girls were on the pier alone Miss McMakin slipped and fell into deep water just beyond Sarah's reach; after a hasty glance around, Sarah whipped off her dress, flung it like a life line to her companion, and drew her to safety.

Here, perhaps, the saga of Sarah Tracy should end, for this was tremendous. It was broad daylight. There were men about the place. So, Sarah being what she was, and the times being what they were, this undressing in public may have been the bravest act of a heroic career.

However, one more touch must be added, if only to establish beyond doubt that this extraordinary creature was human. At last there came a time when even Sarah Tracy's courage failed. It was not until the war was over, but before Miss Cunningham had come back. Suddenly some family crisis demanded Miss McMakin's immediate presence in Philadelphia, and she was compelled to leave in great haste. Then Sarah went to pieces, as is proved by a hasty note dispatched to a neighbor woman, a wild, a downright frantic letter calling the woman to come at once.

For the ultimate terror was upon her. It was not the fear of death. She had been facing that in many forms for four years, death by gunshot, death by artillery fire, death—if she had been caught with Mr. Washington's money—before a firing squad, death at the hands of some murderous bushwhacker, death by pestilence, death by starvation. With the utmost composure she had been strolling arm-in-arm with Death so long that he was a familiar companion. But Mr. Herbert was still on the place, and if the neighbor did not come in hot haste she, Sarah Tracy, would be left overnight without a chaperone, and that she could in no wise endure!

So ends the third star part in the first act of the Mount Vernon drama. Ann Pamela Cunningham, Edward Everett, and Sarah C. Tracy each handled a difficult role to admiration. It is easy to believe that that excellent judge of humanity, George Washington, would have approved them all.

And here is an aside that has nothing to do with the main plot, but that—oh, hear it and then judge. In 1872 Sarah Tracy married Mr. Herbert, and—as far as anyone knows and if there is any justice in this world—they lived happily ever after.

# II. ESTABLISHMENT

he organization that Ann Pamela Cunningham set up to rescue and preserve the home of Washington must be examined in the light of 1853 if it is not to be misunderstood entirely.

It was not democratic. In the climate of opinion prevailing today it is difficult to induce people to accept those four words as a simple statement of fact. They are almost an indictment, for we now take it for granted that what is not democratic must be either fascist or communist. But in 1853 this country had never heard of either fascism or communism, and the opposite of "democratic" was "aristocratic." The Mount Vernon Ladies' Association of the Union was frankly modeled after the aristocratic ideal.

But the model was the genuine ideal, not the sort of pseudo-aristocracy that brought the word into disrepute. Today imagination boggles at the idea of a practical politician's announcing to his constituents, "I am an aristocrat; I love justice and hate equality," but in the generation before Ann Pamela Cunningham's time John Randolph of Roanoke could use those very words and yet win 13 elections. What debased the word here, as elsewhere, was the gradual rise of a self-styled aristocracy that was not composed of the *aristoi*, the best, but largely of persons elevated by the accident of birth, or wealth, or some other circumstance that had nothing to do with excellence.

In assuming that she was competent always to choose the best, the Regent was a little arrogant, that is not to be denied. But the ef-

43

fort was honorable, and if it is impossible to say that her choices were always the best, the record proves beyond a doubt that they were consistently good. The charter gave her, and she exercised firmly, the right to appoint the first group of Vice Regents. Their successors were also to be appointed by the Regent, but they were to be confirmed by the Grand Council, consisting of the Regent and the Vice Regents then in office; and all were to hold office for life.

The Regent was a realist. She knew exactly what she required of the Vice Regents in the several states, to wit, money, but she did not cherish the illusion that they could furnish it out of their own pockets in anything like the sums necessary. So, while a wealthy Vice Regent was desirable, wealth was not by any means the most important qualification. The supremely important thing was the ability to enlist others in the movement both as contributors and as propagandists.

The discovery of even one qualified woman in each state was no simple matter. Tremendous correspondence and long, anxious consultations with all sorts of advisers were involved. To George W. Riggs, treasurer of the Association, she described with precision the ideal Vice Regent:

*The lady should be of a family whose social position would command the confidence of the State, and enable her to enlist the aid of persons of the widest influence. She must be independent, if not of affluent circumstances, as the office is not a salaried one, and attending the annual meetings would involve expense. She must be able to command considerable leisure, as the duties will require much time until the stipulated sums are raised. She should also possess liberal patriotism, energy of character, cultivation of mind, and such a combination of intellectual powers as will ensure that she shall wisely and judicially exercise the power of voting in the Grand Council upon future guardianship and improvement of Mount Vernon.*

Quite a character, this, and one not easily to be found in our own time. Add to the difficulty the extremely withdrawn position of women a hundred years ago, and the task begins to look impossible. Yet by 1858 Miss Cunningham had assembled a list of 22 Vice

*The Vice Regents gather for a portrait at the 1873 Council. Ann Pamela Cunningham (fourth from right) gazes at the Houdon bust of George Washington.*

Regents representing 22 states, plus an "acting" one for the District of Columbia.

If any doubt existed that the first Regent was a very clever woman this list would extinguish it. Remembering always that this was 1858, when a woman's place was emphatically not in the spotlight, one regards with something like awe the very first appointment, Vice Regent Number One, representing the state of Virginia. Her name stands on the roster as "Mrs. Anna Cora Ogden Ritchie," but she was known on two continents as Anna Mowatt, the actress. She was also a poet, playwright, novelist, and essayist, but all that was overshadowed by the fact that she had appeared on the professional stage—incidentally, being good enough to win the acclaim of as sharp a critic as Edgar Allan Poe.

However, there are other facts to be given their due weight before one jumps to the conclusion that Ann Pamela Cunningham had deliberately crashed head-on into all the social prejudices of her time. It

45

is true that as women in general were regarded in 1858, this person had put herself beyond the pale by becoming an actress, but in this case there were other factors to be considered. It was undeniable that she had been born in Ogden, of New Jersey, a granddaughter of the very bellwether of New Jersey aristocrats, that uproarious Reverend Uzal Ogden, whose election as bishop divided the Anglican communion for 14 years, and whose descendants had been judges, governors, and merchant princes ever since. On her mother's side she was a Lewis, descendant of a signer of the Declaration of Independence. Finally, on retiring from the stage she had married a Ritchie of Virginia. Here were family connections that could not be surpassed in America; and, above all, here was a personality of tremendous force. Ann Pamela Cunningham took her, stage acting and all.

But if it was a smart appointment, it was hardly more so than Number Ten, that for Massachusetts, Mrs. Louisa Ingersoll Greenough. The subtlety of this appointment referred not to the individual but to the environment. Counting Edward Everett's fund, Massachusetts had contributed far more money than any other state, and even without Everett more than any other except New York. To an undiscerning person the wife of a Boston millionaire might have seemed a suitable choice to represent this state. But Ann Pamela Cunningham knew better; she chose, instead, the widow of one of the glittering ornaments of Massachusetts culture, Horatio Greenough, the sculptor who had made the colossal statue of Washington facing the Capitol (later removed to the Smithsonian Institution).

The beauty of this choice lay in its implicit suggestion to Massachusetts that more was expected of the Bay State than merely cash. Here was an enterprise that would cost money, to be sure, but that involved intangibles, things of the spirit, including respect for the great past. Horatio Greenough had received recognition in European capitals, particularly Rome, the Mecca of all sculptors, and Massachusetts had shared in the reflected glory. True, in his early days he had subverted the morals of Massachusetts by carving a group of cherubs for James Fenimore Cooper and making them naked. However, that was 20 years in the past and he was now safely dead, so the appointment of his widow was a compliment to the culture of the state that would not have been conferred by the appointment of a woman who had money, but nothing else.

Appointment Number Nine, that of Mary Morris Hamilton, to represent New York, was equally well conceived from the public relations standpoint. Miss Hamilton was a granddaughter of Alexander Hamilton and a niece of Gouverneur Morris, and in addition she was a forthright, energetic character. As it turned out she was a little too vigorous, for during the war years she called a meeting of the Vice Regents on her own responsibility, and her fate was that of the unfortunate Lansing who called a meeting of the Cabinet during Woodrow Wilson's illness—she was never forgiven and soon withdrew. But in the first years she was a tower of strength to the enterprise.

So it went. In practically every state Ann Pamela Cunningham contrived to secure a Vice Regent who was not merely a person but a personage. In the then-frontier state of Wisconsin, for example, her selection was Mrs. Martha Mitchell, wife of Alexander Mitchell, one of the early empire builders, who was even then putting together what became the Chicago, Milwaukee & St. Paul railroad. Today Martha Mitchell is remembered chiefly as the grandmother of General William Mitchell, founder of the American Air Force, but in 1858 she was very much a *grande dame* of the West. In Florida, the Vice Regent was Princess Murat, the American woman who married the son of Napoleon's cavalry commander. Elsewhere the wife of a governor, or a former governor, was appointed, but almost always the woman was a force in herself, regardless of her wealth or social position.

With this personnel it is not surprising that the Association was able to command support, financial, political, and social, throughout the country. What *is* surprising is that Ann Pamela Cunningham herself was able to retain the confidence of the Vice Regents, not only throughout the war, but through the storms of hysteria that swept the country after the war.

Andrew Johnson, President of the United States, had been a stout Union man from the beginning, but he went down in the wild aftermath of the fighting. Ann Pamela Cunningham was not a Secessionist, and she sincerely deplored the break. But she was very definitely a Southerner and frankly gave her first allegiance to South Carolina. She was more vulnerable than the President, yet there seems never to have been any serious effort to replace her as Regent. More convincing evidence of strength of character can hardly be imagined, for an American whose good faith is not questioned even in the backwash of a great war is rare indeed.

In strict fairness, though, some credit should go to the good sense of the Vice Regents. The Regent did not escape without attack; several bitterly partisan letters and articles in newspapers impugned her loyalty, and if the Vice Regents had chosen to do so they could have made things very unpleasant, excusing themselves on the grounds that they were protecting the interests of the Association. To their lasting honor, they did nothing of the sort. They knew Miss Cunningham, and they treated the attacks with the disdain that they deserved. Their main effect, indeed, was to spur several of the Vice Regents to public and passionate defense of their leader.

Their confidence she justified brilliantly during the eight years after her return to Mount Vernon in 1866. The task of physical restoration of the house and grounds was prodigious. During the war extensive work was, of course, out of the question. Herbert had made the place weather tight, but that was about all he could do—and under war conditions that in itself was no trifling accomplishment. But in 1866 a vast deal remained to be done if the processes of decay were to be arrested, and to this huge task Ann Pamela Cunningham devoted all her energy and all her intelligence.

No doubt she welcomed the heavy labor as a distraction from her own miseries; for, like everyone else in her native state, she was financially ruined by the war. Restoring Mount Vernon was difficult, but it was nothing by comparison with the colossal task of restoring South Carolina. Perhaps the use of this work as a means of escape drove her to accomplishments of which she would have been incapable without such a powerful driving force, for her physical disability tended to increase, rather than lessen, with the passage of time.

Along with the engineering work on the building and grounds she pressed the work of refurnishing the place, as nearly as possible as it was furnished when George Washington lived there. One important acquisition had been made before the storm of war burst. It was a harpsichord that had belonged to Nelly Custis, Martha Washington's granddaughter.

This may fairly be described as the happiest of all the acquisitions, for it is associated with the last happy public appearance of the master of the house. Charming Nelly was the apple of the old general's eye, and her wedding to his nephew, Lawrence Lewis, was celebrated on his last birthday, February 22, 1799. Before the year was out, he was dead.

The harpsichord stands in the music room today exactly where it stood when Nelly touched its keys, white then, but since yellowed

*In 1859, Nelly Custis' English harpsichord became the first original furnishing to be returned to Mount Vernon after the Association purchased the estate. The instrument, purchased by George Washington for his stepgranddaughter in 1793, is displayed in the little parlor.*

by time. Mount Vernon has nothing more delightful than the little music room, with its silent reminder that one great life ended as a great life should, attended by youth and beauty and music to the last.

Mary Custis Lee, wife of Robert E. Lee and a great-granddaughter of Martha Washington, was for a long time regarded as the donor of the harpsichord because she sent it on to Mount Vernon from Arlington. But the title to it vested in her cousin, Lorenzo Lewis.

Her son, General George Washington Custis Lee, first lent to the Association, but in 1908 formally transferred as a gift, the relics he had inherited from his grandfather George Washington Parke Custis, including the bed on which George Washington died. Around this piece has been collected through the years practically every article of furniture known to have been in the room in 1799. The visitor is permitted only to look from the doorway into this room, for its contents are too priceless to be risked even in reverent hands.

The collection of the rest of the furnishings proved, however, a long and exacting task. The success it has achieved has been due largely to the diligence, ingenuity, and energy of the Vice Regents. A volume of respectable size could be filled with accounts of Vice Regents in various states who turned detective at the first rumor of some Washington relic in their area, and who, sometimes by using their wiles, sometimes their money, but always their time, their intelligence, and their labor, traced the article down, occasionally to an antique shop, more often to a family mansion, and bore it back triumphantly to Mount Vernon.

Their task was made vastly more difficult, and at the same time more interesting, by Martha Washington's impulsive generosity after her husband's death. Even then the place was a patriotic shrine that countless pilgrims visited, and if Martha took a fancy to

*A prized possession is George Washington's original bed, which was presented to the Association in 1908 by George Washington Custis Lee, great-great-grandson of Martha Washington. Washington died on this bed on December 14, 1799.*

50

a visitor—and she was no misanthrope, she really liked people—nothing would do but he must take away a souvenir. It might be a teaspoon, or a cup and saucer, or some other piece. She was serenely oblivious of the fact that by giving away one she was breaking a set, and in the course of years she not only stripped Mount Vernon of innumerable small objects, but scattered them from end to end of one of the largest countries in the world, for the visitors came from everywhere.

This amiable weakness has made the reassembling of the furnishings a maddening task, yet it has had the effect of adding interest to the search, for a Mount Vernon piece may show up anywhere at any time. To this day no Vice Regent has given up all hope of discovering something in her state that should be at Mount Vernon. A good many things have undoubtedly been destroyed in fires and other accidents, but the Association never gives up as hopelessly lost even those enshrined in libraries and museums in various parts of the country.

In 1873 Ann Pamela Cunningham felt that her work was done. Mount Vernon had been rescued from the danger of commercial exploitation, and the work of restoration was not only well started, but its prosecution was in good hands. Accordingly, at the annual meeting in 1874, she surrendered the Regency to Mrs. Lily M. Berghmans, the original Vice Regent for Pennsylvania, but she resigned her office in a letter that in the minds of her colleagues and successors has displaced the official document issued by the state of Virginia and become the real charter of the Association. It contained an injunction so taken to heart by the members that it is still read at each annual meeting of the Council:

*Ladies, the home of Washington is in your charge—see to it that you keep it the home of Washington! Let no irreverent hand change it; let no vandal hands desecrate it with the fingers of "progress"! Those who go to the home in which he lived and died wish to see in what he lived and died. Let one spot, in this grand country of ours, be saved from change. Upon you rests this duty.*

It was a stern injunction, but the earnestness of the woman who made it compensated for that, solemnly emphasized by the fact that she lived only one year longer. The Mount Vernon Ladies' Association of the Union has been served with devotion and distinction by a long series of Regents—the office is no longer for life, but for a term of five years*—but it is no disparagement of the others to say that none has made the lasting impression of the first of the line.

There is nothing strange in this, for Ann Pamela Cunningham's whole life was consecrated to a single object, which cannot be truthfully said of any of the others. Her physical disability cut her off from most of the normal interests of a woman of her class and time, and the catastrophe of the Civil War very nearly obliterated the society in which she was born. Only Mount Vernon was left, and it absorbed her completely.

But when all this has been said, it does not account for her completely; indeed, it doesn't account for her at all in anything that really matters. There remain the deep mysteries of her courage, her worldly wisdom, and her endurance.

The courage is not uncommon, and it is to the glory of humanity that this can be said. Most men and women fortunate enough to be vigorous and able-bodied admit that they do not understand how anyone can sustain the shock of sudden, permanent disability and ever rise above it; but most of us know someone who has done it and, if there is any sense of proportion in us, are humble in the presence of such a one.

The endurance is less frequently met with, but most of us have seen it. In this case it was extraordinary, but one dare not say unprecedented. The shock of the physical disaster, the long years of weakness punctuated by bouts of savage pain, the second shock of the war and the loss of all that seemed to make life worth living, and the dragging slowness with which the great objective was approached, combine to make a rather dreadful total, but no doubt others have endured as much or worse.

But endurance added to courage and then shrewdness added to

*The term of Regent was reduced to three years in 1973; each Regent is eligible for re-election to one additional term.

both in a single personality make a total that is rare indeed. Yet this ailing recluse from a remote Southern plantation proceeded from start to finish with an assurance of step, a deftness of touch, an accuracy in reading character that a wily politician, a Talleyrand, a Metternich, might have observed with astonishment and envy.

She could handle them all. Whether it was a skeptical Petigru, an emotional, generous Everett, a hard-boiled banker, like George W. Riggs, or a wrathful, embittered planter like John Augustine Washington, she bent them to her will and made them like it. What is, to a man at least, most amazing of all, she could assemble a couple of dozen women, each a vigorous personality in her own right—including, indeed, some of the most vigorous feminine personalities in all America—bend them to her will and make *them* like it.

She had her faults, of course. Her shockingly slight appreciation of the true worth of Sarah Tracy, for example, indicates a moral blind spot that cannot be quite forgiven, and her treatment of Mary Morris Hamilton looks, in the perspective of 80 years, more than questionable. But it must not be forgotten that Miss Hamilton was no meek and mousy little creature; she was able, very well able, to take care of herself, and she may have landed some terrific blows of which we know nothing.

But when all this is admitted, the fact remains that this was not merely a remarkable woman, but a remarkable human being regardless of sex. Ann Pamela Cunningham stands as a shattering disproof of the old idea of a Southern lady as charming but brainless and not to be taken seriously in any of the serious affairs of life. For that, she should be gratefully remembered by all women who have suffered under that blight.

Yet the duty she laid upon her successors has not been discharged without incessant effort. Irreverent hands and vandal hands have been kept off, but unfortunately they are not the only forces of change, and Father Time is vastly more formidable than human hands. Wind and weather, frost and sunshine, mildew and termites work constantly to destroy the creations of men and to combat them is no easy task.

Then Mount Vernon was still further exposed by its very nature.

The first reason for preserving it was to make it an inspiration to each succeeding generation, and how could it inspire unless it were seen? To shut it up behind high walls and locked gates would have been to destroy its greatest value. The people must be admitted, but the very presence of enormous crowds is destructive, be they ever so well-conducted.

Imagine taking Patton's Army and marching it, under the strictest discipline, through an ordinary residence. The men might not touch one single thing with evil intent; nevertheless, there would not be much house left after a million of them had marched through.

Yet the equivalent of this—more than a million every year—does happen, and the house stands because and only because strenuous, incessant efforts combat the wear and tear upon it.

The river itself, the same vast river that gives the situation its magnificence, is a sleepless enemy. Even in Washington's time the danger was evident. The Potomac had undercut the bluff to such an extent that the family tomb was in danger, and Washington himself chose the spot for a new vault and drew plans for its construction. Death intervened before he could complete it, but his heirs followed out the plans and removed the bodies of George and Martha Washington to the new tomb in 1831.

However, the old tomb is still intact because a powerful stone revetment now controls the force of the current. It is one bit of construction that nobody notices, for it is invisible except from the river, but the way it came into being illustrates one way in which the Association sometimes operates. Some 50 years ago small landslides made it clear that the danger of a serious collapse was imminent. Army engineers examined the site and decided that a retaining wall was essential, but at a minimum the work would cost $15,000 and there simply wasn't that much money in the treasury. Yet the danger was pressing and was increasing every day.

In this situation the Vice Regent for California spoke up, saying, in effect, "We can't sit around until we have collected the money, for the bank may have caved by that time. Go ahead with the work and send me the bill." She was Mrs. Phoebe Apperson

Hearst, wife of a senator from California and mother of William Randolph Hearst, the newspaper publisher.

This was a huge gift for an individual, the largest up to that time, but it was not unprecedented. Fifteen years earlier, when the entrance gates were in danger of falling to pieces, Mrs. Mitchell of Wisconsin had had them repaired at her own expense, and in 1878, when a burglar alarm system was needed and funds were low, the Vice Regent for New York, Mrs. Justine Van Rensselaer Townsend, met the bill.

These gifts are memorable because of their size, but not because they were made by Vice Regents. There was hardly a meeting of the Council, especially in the early years, at which half the membership could not report gifts of some sort, some of them of small intrinsic value but on account of their historical associations priceless.

The Association was fortunate, also, in that the national character of its work brought it generous support from patriotic citizens in no way connected with it. For instance, in 1908, after Congress had refused to appropriate $20,000 for the purchase of the dress sword that Washington wore when he resigned his commission as general in 1783, and when he was inaugurated as first President of the United States in 1789, the sword was purchased and presented to the Association by a private citizen, J. Pierpont Morgan, the elder. Fifteen years later, the sash that belongs with the sword was in like manner bought and given to the Association by the second J. Pierpont Morgan.

In 1924 the Council was worried over its obsolete fire-fighting equipment; and when word of it reached him the most modern, motor-driven apparatus was presented by Henry Ford. Years before that the ladies had struggled with the problem of lighting the grounds electrically for protection against prowlers. That was long before power lines had been strung across Virginia, so designs for an individual power system were drawn and presented to the Association by no less an electrical engineer than Thomas A. Edison.

Electric lighting, it should perhaps be mentioned, is confined to

*Phoebe Apperson Hearst, mother of newspaper publisher William Randolph Hearst, served as Vice Regent for California from 1889 to 1918.*

56

the grounds and subsidiary buildings. The house itself is never lighted except on very special occasions, and then by low voltage batteries.* There is no electric wiring in it except that connected with elaborate fire and burglar alarm systems. The even temperature necessary to the preservation of old furniture and fabrics is maintained by a modern heating plant located far enough from the house to eliminate the risk of fire from that source.

Inevitably some mistakes were made in the early days. All sorts of objects were gratefully accepted and installed in the mansion under the impression that they had belonged to Washington when—as later investigation revealed—they had no connection with him whatever. Others, perfectly authentic as far as their connection with Washington is concerned, had no relation to Mount Vernon. The great majority of the Washington portraits, for example, never hung in Mount Vernon and have no rightful place there, nor have the state papers, nor even as significant a document as Washington's commission as general. They appertain to the commander in chief or to the first President of the United States, rather than to the master of Mount Vernon, and are appropriately housed elsewhere.

But the establishment of the place as an accurate picture of the home life of the Father of His Country proceeded rapidly under Mrs. Berghmans until her death in 1891, and for the next 20 years under Mrs. Townsend of New York, third Regent. The mistakes were all minor, and most of them of a kind that could easily be corrected. In the major phases of the project there was no mistake.

They included some remarkably arduous undertakings, for Ann Pamela Cunningham's injunction—"let one spot in this grand country of ours be saved from change"—involved a certain self-contradiction. Mount Vernon was changed, tremendously changed, in being transformed from the home of a Virginia country gentleman into a patriotic shrine, and this change necessarily involved others.

---

*A state-of-the-art lighting system that simulates the light levels of candles and fires was installed in 1986.

One, strange to say, was an artificial change in the geological formation of the hill itself. For years repeated landslides made it seem hopeless to keep the hill in anything like its shape at the end of the 18th century, but once again the engineers came to the rescue, civilian engineers this time. By a long series of test borings and scientific measurements of drainage, they determined that under a thick bed of clay that is the top of the hill lies a stratum of sand that alternately becomes water-soaked and then drained. The cure obviously was artificial drainage of this stratum, which the engineers effected by driving tunnels into the hill almost at the level of the river. They thought at first that 150 feet or so of tunneling would do the work, but before they finished, the drainage system was 401 feet long.

So here is one way in which Mount Vernon is definitely changed—it is more solid than it ever was in George Washington's day. But the change was made in order to avoid changes in its superficial aspect.

A quarter of a mile below the Mansion—that is, down river—there was originally a pestilential marsh that the outspoken Washington described as "Hell Hole." It was a breeding place of mosquitoes and was largely responsible for the plagues of chills and fever with which Sarah Tracy had so much trouble.

But Hell Hole now is a few level acres serving as the nursery and seed-bed for the gardens of the estate. Here the early plants, vegetables and flowers, are started and here shrubbery and young trees are grown to keep the hedges and groves in perfect shape. The change was effected by Mrs. Hearst's retaining wall supplemented by drainage planned by the engineers.

Perhaps, though, the most remarkable effect of permanence achieved by incessant changes in detail is presented by the gardens that lie on either side of the broad lawn—the bowling green—on the west side of the house. To the right, as one stands in the doorway, lies the flower garden, to the left the kitchen garden, both screened from view by trees and high brick walls.

It is safe to say that George Washington never saw such perfect gardens in all his life, but they are exactly the kind of gardens he planned and tried to create. If they are better, it is simply because gardeners have learned better methods of cultivation, propagation, and fertilization than were known in his time.

In the kitchen garden, for example, the tomatoes are represented by small, pear-shaped objects, hardly recognizable as tomatoes. Purists have objected that even these should not be there because long after Washington's day the "love-apple" was regarded by most people as poisonous. But the botanists have found that in Italy and Spain tomatoes were used in salads as early as 1600; they have found a letter, dated 1742, in which an Englishman advised a Virginia friend to plant tomatoes; and they have found it recorded that Thomas Jefferson put them in at Monticello as early as 1781. The large, juicy fruit of modern times, however, was unknown, so only its small, early prototype appears at Mount Vernon. On the other hand, the orange trees in the greenhouse at the side of the flower garden are as good as any; for in the 18th century practically every great estate in Europe and many in America had an orangery.

The flower beds have no hybrid tea roses, for there was no such thing until 1867, and certain wall fruits are espaliered, although there are modern varieties that come to perfection without such treatment. No exact account of every flower in the gardens has ever been found; so whatever is known to have been common in Virginia gardens in George Washington's day is accepted at Mount Vernon, on the theory that he might have had it, and there is no assurance that he did not.

A feature of the flower gardens, aside from their luxuriance, that astonishes the modern visitor is their enclosure, and about this there is debate. The high brick wall was certainly put there by Washington. The box was also planted by him. But did he have the high transverse hedges that now divide the whole area into what are, in effect, separate gardens, or was it all open?

In the 18th century box was used both as a border and as a hedge. Around the individual flower beds the box was certainly kept trimmed down to six inches or so; otherwise their formal designs—fleur-de-lis, lozenges, spirals and the like—would not have been perceptible. Most of the box at Mount Vernon was planted in 1798, and as it is slow growing it could not have reached its present height in Washington's lifetime.

But this does not rule out the possibility that the present closed effect is correct, for he might have had something else that he used for screening. It is certain that in 18th-century formal gardens privacy was sought. The conditions of life in the great houses made it desirable, for with the constant presence of visitors, and the great numbers of servants necessary when everything was done by hand, privacy indoors was almost unobtainable. Therefore a secluded walk in the garden must have been a sanctuary at the end of a long summer day to a man and woman who had struggled many hours with the affairs of a large estate; while without doubt it breathed romance to young people.

As a matter of fact, it breathes romance today, especially to anyone who can see it in the late afternoon, or the early morning, when the air is heavy with the scent of box and of the old-fashioned flowers—lavender and heliotrope, lilies, pinks, phlox, ragged robin, canterbury bell, musk roses, celsiana, columbine, sweet William, and more others than you can count. Such gardens Jane Austen peopled with well-conducted but luckless persons, and Robert Herrick, before her, with persons not so well-conducted, and before him an infinite line of poets and romancers, back to the "garden enclosed" of Canticles. Nothing about Mount Vernon evokes "the tender grace of a day that is dead" more strongly than the flower gardens.

Just beyond then is an evocation of a very different kind. Here stood the slave quarters, and they have been restored as carefully as the gardens and with what the squeamish may regard as ruthless accuracy. "There is not a man living who wishes more sincerely than I do to see a plan adopted for the abolition of slavery," said George Washington, not in a public address devoted to conventional sentiments, but in a private letter to his friend Robert Morris, but the greatest man is to some extent the slave of his times. All the testimony agrees that Washington was a good master, but the ineradicable barbarity of the institution was too much for the best of masters. The silent testimony of the quarters is more eloquent than the loudest denunciations of the abolitionists.

Yet "in what he lived" this was an important part, and to omit it would be to falsify the record, but the record of any great man should be presented as a whole, if later generations are to appreciate him at his true worth. The visitor, standing at the east front of Mount Vernon, surveying the panorama of the noble river, describing its great arc around the foot of the hill, with the tranquil green hills of Maryland beyond, can hardly escape the impression that here is an appropriate setting for a great life. He may even drift into a cynical mood, asking himself who, indeed, with this before him, would not have developed a broad view of the world, would not have been inspired to broaden his thoughts and lift the level of his deeds? So he may be inclined a little to cheapen the achievement of Washington.

It is not amiss, therefore, to have this reminder that the environment of the man was far from ideal, that he had to fight his way up even as you and I against social and economic forces that tended to drag him down. It would be a great disservice, especially to the younger generation, to present Washington's environment as Parson Weems tried to present his character, flawless and irreproachable from every standpoint. That would put an end to emulation, for who can hope to rival a demigod? Who can hope to live after the fashion of a man who lived in an environment of exquisite perfection?

Mount Vernon was not the Elysian Fields where the Blessed walk in eternal calm through meads of asphodel. It was a human habitation, where a human being struggled with difficulties very much like those that you and I encounter—the uncontrollable seasons, the stubbornness of the refractory earth, human incompetence and indolence and error, and all the monstrous evils that afflicted the times. Yet this human being, loaded with some burdens, as, for example, the institution of slavery, from which you and I are happily free, triumphed over all the difficulties and emerged a figure of heroic mold.

That is the message of Mount Vernon. If you and I find it somewhat cold comfort, it is an indication that we haven't in us the stuff that Washington had, and so much the worse for us.

# III. REFINEMENT

he successive phases of the work of the Mount Vernon Ladies' Association shaded into each other so gradually that it is impossible to fix the time at which one ended and the next began, but it is roughly accurate to date the third stage from about the period of the first World War. Perhaps one may say that the work of establishment was finished with the Regency of Mrs. Townsend, who resigned in 1909 and died in 1912, and that the work of refinement began with her successor, Miss Harriet Clayton Comegys of Delaware, who became the fourth Regent in 1909 and held the office for 18 years.

This refinement is simply the work of bringing the house and grounds ever closer to their exact condition at the time of Washington's death. Martha Washington survived her husband by only three years, dying in 1802, and between her death and the acquisition of the property by the Association there was a hiatus of more than 50 years, during which the property was in private hands. With the best will in the world the heirs could not maintain the place in its original condition. The first of them, Bushrod Washington, necessarily gave his first attention to his duties as an Associate Justice of the Supreme Court, which left him little time for the management of an estate; in any event, there is no evidence that Justice Washington was a particularly good estate manager.

On the other hand, there is definite evidence that neither the first nor the second John Augustine Washington had anything like

George Washington's ability in handling farm land and farm labor. While it was in their control the fertility of the estate and its financial return steadily dwindled. By the time he sold, the second one of that name, if not definitely bankrupt, was in financial straits that were rapidly becoming intolerable.

To do them justice, both these proprietors were in an impossible situation. They and their families were like people living in a museum, which they had to maintain at their own expense. The stream of visitors to Washington's home was incessant, and the hospitality that the Virginian code imposed upon the owners was a heavy drain on their resources. It was too heavy. In view of the mounting expenses and the shriveling revenue from the estate, they found it impossible to make even the most necessary repairs. Outbuildings not only fell into decay but in many cases disappeared. Fire gutted the greenhouse, and the gaunt ruins of its brick walls alone were left in 1853. Gradually the gardens became desolate, weeds invaded the lawns, wind and lightning played havoc with the groves and the destroyed trees could not be replaced, broken furniture had to be discarded. Of the long row of chairs that Washington made a feature of the piazza on the east front only one was left—the more regrettable as it was his favorite spot for entertaining callers in fine weather, including those who came on serious business. Many conferences of vast importance in the history of the nation were held on that piazza by statesmen sitting in those chairs.

Finally, the furniture in the place comprised John Augustine Washington's household goods. He had to take it with him when he moved out, for it was in everyday use; and besides, with the heirlooms from George Washington were mingled all kinds of objects acquired in the nearly two generations that had elapsed since his death.

This circumstance complicated enormously the Association's work, especially in the first few years. All sorts of people showed up with all sorts of articles, some of which had indubitably come from Mount Vernon, but had been placed there by Bushrod Washington, or his successors. When the person in question was a generous enthusiast, offering the article as a gift, it was difficult to refuse; and when he was an antique dealer demanding a stiff price, it was not always possible to discriminate. The records then were by no means as accurate and complete as they became later. In those early days the Association spent considerable sums on articles that subsequent research proved had never belonged to George Washington, perhaps had never been seen by him.

In some instances no deception, not even self-deception, was involved. For instance, it was known that in Washington's day a sundial had stood on the bowling green, and plans existed showing its position accurately, but there was no trace of the dial nor any detailed description of it. But there had been a sundial on the spot, so in 1889, the Vice Regent for Rhode Island, Mrs. Abby Wheaton Chace, raised funds in her state for a sundial mounted on a red granite base designed by a noted architect and with a plate engraved by a celebrated silversmith. Nobody pretended that it was a replica of the one Washington had, but it was a sundial and it made a handsome ornament on the lawn. Years later, however, someone rummaging through old papers turned up a description of Washington's dial, mounted simply on a "twisted locust post." Then the plate was found in the possession of one of his heirs and was purchased by the Vice Regent for Connecticut, Miss Jennings. Immediately down came the magnificent Rhode Island gift, to be replaced by one far more meager, but correct to the last detail.

Then there was the "Louis XVI carpet" that was spread for some time on the dining room floor, but that is now rolled up and tucked away in storage. The seemingly well-authenticated story was that Louis XVI had the carpet woven at Aubusson for the first president, with the arms of the United States included in the pattern. The whole legend fell to pieces when records turned up showing that Washington, not the King of France, had had it woven, not in Aubusson, but in Philadelphia, not for Mount Vernon, but for the presidential mansion. So a cherished possession was instantly removed, even though it had historical value of its own as one of the first fine carpets woven in America.

*The infamous "Louis XVI" carpet was displayed in the large dining room in the 1930s and 1940s, but was removed when it was discovered that the carpet, though valuable, had been made for the presidential mansion in Philadelphia and had never been used at Mount Vernon.*

If this attention to detail seems to verge upon the fanatical, let the reader remember that Mount Vernon exists to remind us of a man whose most conspicuous characteristic was his absolute integrity. Of all the great Americans, Washington is the one most completely clear of any suggestion of the fraudulent, the make-believe, the phony. We have had more brilliant men, we have had more pious men, we have had shrewder men, but the country has yet to produce a more genuine man than its first president. In the place that is to preserve his memory, therefore, no effort is too great to assure that the smallest detail shall be exactly what it pretends to be.

Yet the Association has not committed itself to a slavish devo-

66

tion to the letter that killeth, ignoring the spirit that giveth life. There was, for example, the problem of "the Lafayette room," the bedchamber occupied by Lafayette when he visited his old commander. Not a stick of the furniture that was in that room at the time of the Marquis's visit has been recovered. It is probable that it has been destroyed, and it is almost certain that if any of it still exists it could not be authenticated after all these years. Yet an absolutely bare room would in itself strike a false note, which is not to be considered. The Association accordingly has furnished the room with pieces authentically of the period, but the visitor is carefully informed that this is not the original, merely the best approximation possible.

There is, however, one incongruous exception to the lack of pretense at Mount Vernon, one that no visitor can overlook. It is the outside wall of the house itself—of wood, but cut in such a manner as apparently to imitate stone. It is hard for the ordinary visitor to make this fit the character of a man who in everything else was conspicuous for his respect for the genuine, so it is perhaps worth a little detailed attention.

At the time that George Washington enlarged the home that his father had built, and for half a century thereafter, this method of treating outer walls was fashionable in America. It was a frank imitation of the European style of masonry known as "rustication," but the intent was not to deceive. It was to achieve the effect sought by European stonemasons, who beveled the edges of the blocks to break the monotony of plain ashlar. The sunlight of Virginia is both more abundant and more intense than that of England, so rustication of a white-painted wooden wall in Virginia is even better justified than similar treatment of a stone wall in England.

Mount Vernon is somewhat unusual in that the rustication is carried all the way up. The commoner practice was to restrict it to the lower story with a smooth surface above, but this isolated building presented a different problem from that of a house on a city street, and Washington may have felt that this expensive treatment was worthwhile not to give the impression of a stone building but to achieve a more pleasant effect by breaking the glare of sunlight on a flat, white wall.

Today it is unusual, at least in the eastern states, for a house as large as Mount Vernon to be built entirely of wood, and many of us have lost familiarity with really skillful carpentry. This accounts for the astonishment with which we regard the walls of Mount Vernon, but the contemporary observer no doubt saw nothing odd in it and certainly nothing spurious, but merely an example of a highly popular, if somewhat new style. His verdict would have been the equivalent of our "very modern."

It may be argued, though, that this style of construction does illustrate one facet of Washington's character that has not often been emphasized. His conservatism was political and philosophical, not social. Like Theodore Roosevelt a century later, he adhered to "the old moralities" but he never adhered to the old fashions. In everything of secondary importance—dress, house furnishings, equipage, etiquette—he liked to appear strictly up to date. His letters to his factors are filled with admonitions to be sure that whatever they purchased for him was in the latest fashion.

So if rustication happened to be in favor at the moment, as it was, the fact that it was a relatively recent innovation would have been a recommendation rather than an objection in the eyes of George Washington. His taste was sound enough to prevent his acceptance of anything wildly fantastic, but he was no hidebound worshiper of the old merely because it was old. Thus he made Mount Vernon a remarkable example of the best in the manners and customs of his day, and it has been the endeavor of the Association to maintain it in exactly that character.

The Association, of course, does not hesitate to employ modern methods and materials where they do not alter the appearance of the building. Steel, for example, has been used for extra strengthening wherever necessary and where it does not show. The cornerstone, having begun to deteriorate, was removed and the surface given a highly modern chemical treatment to harden the relatively soft sandstone and make it impervious to the weather.

The one Windsor chair remaining from the dozens originally on the great piazza was taken to a skillful modern chairmaker, who copied it with faithful precision. So the row of chairs today looks exactly as it did when the Founding Fathers occupied them and discussed with the master of Mount Vernon the construction, not of a chair, but of a country.

In 1914 the flagstone floor on which the chairs stood was in bad condition. It was known that Washington had imported the flags from England, but their origin was unknown.

The Geological Museum in London solved this problem. A fragment of one of the broken stones was taken there and promptly identified as having come from a sandstone quarry at St. Bees, so 1500 stones of the same size and shape were ordered to repair the floor. Incidentally, the United States Treasury Department showed less friendly interest than the British Geological Museum; it insisted on collecting duty on the flagstones, regardless of the fact that they were not to be sold in this country, but were to repair a national shrine.

The work of refinement was greatly facilitated by the fact that George Washington was a surveyor, skilled in platting and exact in his measurements. Among his papers were many designs, executed with draughtsman's skill, showing the arrangement of the house and grounds. A particularly interesting one shows not only the meandering driveways on the two sides of the lawn, but the exact location of each of the hundred or so trees bordering the drive, with a notation of the species of each tree.

There is some question among the authorities as to whether this plat shows the trees as they actually existed, or as Washington proposed to have them. But it has been accepted as a guide and is consulted whenever it becomes necessary to replace a tree. When the property was acquired and for years thereafter the northeast corner of the lawn was bare. But then someone discovered, not in the Washington papers, but in a letter written by one of his visitors, a long description of Mount Vernon mentioning especially the writer's delight in the beautiful locust grove on the northeast corner. Today more than a dozen large locust trees shade the spot.

One of the great individual contributions to the preservation of Mount Vernon was the work of Dr. Charles Sprague Sargent, creator of the Arnold Arboretum at Harvard and doubtless the most distinguished arboriculturist America has yet produced. For 13 years, from 1914 until his death in 1927, the trees of Mount Vernon received his personal care. Like the gardens, they are certainly in far better condition today than they were in Washington's time, but they are the same kind of trees, and they are growing where he had them.

The lawns are a different matter. The Association has been content only to determine exactly where Washington had green lawns and to see to it that green lawns are there now. But the grasses are selected for their survival value, not because they were known to Washington. This is necessary, because the modern lawns must take such pounding as the original ones never had to endure. Incessant attention and the most modern methods of nourishing, watering, and reseeding are required to keep them in existence at all. To attempt to go back to the old varieties and the old practices would simply wipe the lawns out altogether.

Within the house, too, there is one frank, undisguised anomaly. Along the path that the visitors follow through the rooms the floors are covered with the thickest, stoutest, rubber tile floor covering that modern manufacturers can turn out.* Nothing else could stand the beating at all, and the covering has to be constantly renewed.

So the apparent tranquil changelessness of Mount Vernon is something of an illusion. It is the result of ceaseless straining battle against the forces of time and decay. Only the resources of modern science and technology have made possible the preservation of the place as it looked in Washington's time.

*The Windsor chairs on the piazza were carefully recreated from an original chair owned by George Washington. When the flagstone floor of the piazza needed repair, the Association tracked down the sandstone quarry in England that had provided the original stone to order replacements.*

*now industrial-grade carpeting.

One other force has contributed, although the extent of its contribution is appreciated only by the staff directly in charge of the work. This is the force of public criticism which, especially within the past several decades, has become extremely alert and informed. Since the wars of the 20th century began there has been a vast amount of research in the Revolutionary period, attended by the development of specialists in every phase of the life of the early republic. One effect of this has been an astonishing increase in the knowledge and vigilance of the visitors to Mount Vernon.

Time was when almost any sort of anomaly might stand in the rooms unnoticed for an indefinite period, but that is true no longer. The tests for authenticity that the Association gives any piece offered for display are rigid, but they are only the beginning. If there is the slightest question it will be raised very soon after the article, whatever it may be, is installed. Here is, let us say, a piece of silverware attributed to some well-known craftsman of the late 18th century; hardly will it be set in place before some authority on the silversmiths of the period comes through and begins to ask pointed questions—the design is characteristic, yes, but did the craftsman actually adopt that design before the year 1801? If he did not, then the piece, if it ever was at Mount Vernon, must have been brought there by Bushrod Washington or one of his successors, not by George.

Then begins a dogged search through all that is recorded about that silversmith and his work. Perhaps it may be established that the man did begin to use that design first in 1801, and if so, the piece will be removed. But perhaps a cross reference will lead the searcher to some old books of memoirs, or the "Letters and Papers" of a forgotten statesman, or of a lady of quality, with a line to the effect that, "at Mr. X's shop today I bought a silver compote dish with the design of—" whatever the design happens to be. If the date of the letter is, say, 1796, then the criticism fails.

Members of the staff are constantly being astonished by the extent and accuracy of the curious lore that the American public has picked up. There is nothing so obscure or so trivial that somebody has not studied it diligently and deeply, and that somebody is pretty sure to visit Mount Vernon eventually. He may have made a special study of doorknobs, or andirons, or saucepans, or varnishes. He may know little or nothing about anything else, but if there is something out of line in his specialty he will spot it instantly and remark on it. This has happened often enough to justify the statement that the general public has made an important contribution to the refining process.

That process still goes on, and will continue indefinitely. Mount Vernon is not perfect and will never be perfect, for there is no such thing as a perfect reproduction of the past. But it is closer to perfection today than it ever was before, and it moves steadily toward that unattainable goal.

While old James Louis Petigru was amply justified in insisting on including the word "ladies" in the name of the Association because it is they who have done the work, the story of Mount Vernon for the past century certainly should include the names of at least four men. These are Upton H. Herbert, James McHenry Hollingsworth, Harrison H. Dodge, and Charles C. Wall, the four Superintendents of the estate.[*]

The position of Superintendent[†] at Mount Vernon calls for as wide a diversity of talents as can well be imagined. The Superintendent must be, if not exactly a farmer, yet a man acquainted with soils, seasons, and the proper handling of growing plants; while at the same time he must be, if not exactly a theatrical producer, yet a man acquainted with the principles of dramatic display, with the handling of large crowds, and the proper conduct of a box office.

In between, he needs some knowledge of engineering, of carpentry and masonry, and of every detail of a domestic establish-

[*] For a full listing of the Superintendents/Resident Directors since 1858, please see the appendix.
[†] now called Resident Director.

ment, from polishing silver and dusting furniture to dietetics and budgeting. Obviously, he must be a reasonably competent accountant, but he must also be a better than mediocre antiquarian and an excellent historian at least of the last half of the 18th century. If he is to be brilliantly successful he should add to all this the tact and shrewdness of a first-rate ambassador, for he deals with all types of humanity, many of them with something to sell.

In recent years the Superintendent at Mount Vernon has been able to employ experts in many of these lines to whom he can entrust their various specialties. But, as every business executive learns, if the man at the top doesn't know something about everything, the best staff of experts ever assembled will get out of hand and confusion will result.

The good fortune of the Association in its Superintendents is attested by the fact that none of them served for less than 10 years, while the Grand Old Man of the group, Harrison H. Dodge, held the post from 1885 to his death in 1937, a term of 52 years. Herbert, the first Superintendent, served for ten years, Hollingsworth for 13, while the incumbent has been on duty for 16. As a matter of fact, Mr. Wall's* service is longer, for he served under Mr. Dodge for eight years before succeeding him.

As to exactly what the Mount Vernon Ladies' Association of the Union has done in the first hundred years of its existence, opinions are as various as the people who express them. The Association has preserved and restored approximately to the original state the house and grounds of a famous man. That material fact is accepted by all,

*Charles Cecil Wall retired in 1976, after 47 years of service to Mount Vernon. Adding this to Mr. Dodge's 52-year tenure (with which Mr. Wall overlapped eight years), Mount Vernon had only two Resident Superintendents/Directors in a span of 91 years. This opportunity is all the more remarkable when one considers that Mr. Dodge served under a Regent and 13 Vice Regents who had been appointed by Ann Pamela Cunningham.

but when you pass beyond the physical fact and ask for the meaning of the work, you may find almost anything.

"It's a cozy little place," said Queen Elizabeth II of England.

"Here is the heart of America," said a distinguished Frenchman. They were both right. So was Washington himself when he described it as "a well-resorted tavern," and so was Edward Everett when he intoned, "grateful children of America will make their pilgrimage to it as to a shrine." Many do just that, and many others come out from Washington in the holiday spirit in which they visit the city's parks. Schoolchildren come by hundreds of thousands and some are impressed, while others no doubt regard it merely as a grand break in the monotony of classes.

But queen or stenographer, emperor or schoolboy, they are all shown the same thing and left to make what they can of it. Here is the environment in which George Washington lived and died; what it meant to him, you are free to guess; what it means to you, you are free to ponder. The Association has told the tale, but it appends no moral.

The tale itself, however, shatters the delusion that the United States is a land without traditions or an accepted code. The order, tranquility, and grace of Mount Vernon are not the creation of the ingenious artificers of the atom bomb, but have been our heritage from days beyond the birth of the republic. The United States of America was endowed with them from the beginning.

It is significant, too, that this part of our national heritage was not rescued and preserved for us by the rulers of the state, but by a popular movement; it is doubly significant that this movement was instituted and carried through to success by American women. Ann Pamela Cunningham was an extraordinary character, to be sure, but she was completely feminine and completely American, so much so that it has been easy for her successors to understand her ideal, and possible, if far from easy, to sustain, extend, and perfect her work.

The beautiful home on the Potomac has stood as a monument to George Washington since the day he died, but since 1853 it has also commemorated the patriotism, the energy, and the intelligence of the American woman.

# EPILOGUE

ith the publication of *Mount Vernon: The Story of a Shrine* in 1953, the Mount Vernon Ladies' Association looked back over its first hundred years, a century of hard work and achievement set in motion by the vision of one woman. The story begins with Ann Pamela Cunningham, who took up the cause of saving Mount Vernon with an extraordinary faith in the permanence of her work. "You would regard me as an enthusiast, a dreamer," she once wrote to a Vice Regent, "unless like myself the present had receded from you and you...saw and felt...as those will see and feel who live a century hence." Now well into its second century, the Mount Vernon Ladies' Association is still guided by its founder's vision as it carries forward her mission to "keep Mount Vernon the home of Washington."

The Association's 1953 centennial proved to be more than the celebration of a traditional milestone. While the Ladies reflected on the achievements of the past, they did not pause, even briefly, to rest on their laurels. With their second century began a new era that would bring challenges and opportunities beyond even Miss Cunningham's dreams.

## THE MANSION

Since the beginning, the Mansion has been the centerpiece of the Association's restoration efforts. In the earliest days, the very survival of the building was at stake, as the Association struggled to make major repairs. Over the decades, the recovery of original furnishings, ongoing research and advances in preservation technology have brought the house ever closer to its appearance during Washington's lifetime. Gerald Johnson termed this gradual and painstaking work in the modern period a "refinement of the restoration." By definition, this refinement continues indefinitely, as each generation brings its own perspective and expertise to build upon the work of its predecessors.

Mount Vernon is the most complete surviving example of an 18th-century plantation, and it is the best documented. While the evolution of the estate through the many generations of Washington family ownership is thoroughly studied and recorded, the restoration focuses on a single year, 1799. This, the last year of George Washington's life, marks the highest point of the estate's development.

In addition, there is also a 1799 inventory of the contents of the Mansion that was taken by the appraisers of Washington's estate after his death on December 14 of that year. This room-by-room record, along with information taken from Washington's correspondence, accounts, visitors' descriptions and other contemporary sources, provide the basis for the current Mansion furnishing plan.

The execution of the plan is an evolutionary process, as original furnishings, once widely scattered, are returned, and appropriate period pieces are acquired to fill in what is missing. Since the Association's centennial in 1953, several major acquisitions have allowed a more authentic presentation of the rooms.

Often these acquisitions have been made only after decades of curatorial patience and detective work. One stunning example was the reinstallment of two sideboards in the large dining room, more than a century-and-a-half after the original pair had been removed. George Washington owned a matching pair of sideboards that were made for him by the noted Philadelphia cabinetmaker, John Aitken, in 1797. At the end of the presidency, Washington brought them back to Mount Vernon where they were displayed on either side of the grand Palladian window in his recently-completed large dining room.

After Martha Washington's death in 1802, the Aitken sideboards were separated. One of the original pair, which remained in the possession of Mrs. Washington's descendants, was returned to Mount Vernon in 1873. The second sideboard, it is believed, was purchased by Robert Peter, Jr., the brother-in-law of Martha Washington's granddaughter, Martha Custis Peter, at a private family sale in 1802. It has since disappeared without a trace.

For nearly a century the Association searched for the missing sideboard, displaying its mate in the small dining room in the place of yet another sideboard table owned by Washington, which has also been lost to history.

In the spring of 1966, a sideboard nearly identical to the one at Mount Vernon was discovered in a private collection in New Jersey. The Association was able to purchase the piece, which was found in a structural analysis to have also come from the shop of John Aitken. Although there appears to be no other historical connection between the two sideboards, their overall dimensions conform within an inch.

The only discernible difference is the design of the oval inlaid medallions on the front of each piece; the original Mount Vernon sideboard bears a single stylized flower, while its cousin displays an oak and acorn motif.

The acquisition of this remarkable match allowed the Association to return the original sideboard, once again as part of a pair, to the large dining room, a critical step in the furnishing plan. The following year, a period sideboard table, approximating what is believed to be the long-lost piece that Washington kept in the small dining room, was purchased from a dealer in England to be displayed in that room.

Among other acquisitions contributing to the authenticity of the rooms is a rare 18th-century Windsor fan chair purchased by the Association in 1982. Evidently, George Washington saw and admired such a contraption while in Philadelphia attending the Constitutional Convention in 1787. The record shows that he purchased one and had it shipped to Mount Vernon, where it remained in his study until after his death. Although Washington's original fan chair has disappeared, the period piece, one of only two surviving examples, stands in its place in the study, to the delight of the visitors.

The artwork throughout the Mansion is original or representa-

*The Association strives for authenticity in restoring the Mansion to its 18th-century appearance. In the large dining room, a missing sideboard from a pair owned by George Washington was replaced with another 18th-century sideboard by the same maker. Today the original and its substitute mate have been returned to the Mansion, where they are displayed on either side of the Palladian window.*

tive of the original paintings, drawings and prints that Washington displayed. One interesting recent addition is a sketch of the demolition of the Bastille that had been sent to Washington, along with the key to the famous French prison, by the Marquis de Lafayette in 1790. Although the key is one of the few original pieces that remained at Mount Vernon when the Association purchased the estate in 1858, the sketch was taken by the Washington family and sold at auction in the late 19th century. Its whereabouts were unknown for almost a century when, in 1987, the Association learned that it was part of a private individual's estate. The Bastille sketch is now on loan to Mount Vernon, hanging once again in its original place below the key in the central passage.

At times the refinement of the restoration has involved the removal rather than the addition of furnishings. In 1978, to the disappointment of many visitors, a handsome tall clock was taken down from the central staircase landing where it had been displayed for generations. Although the piece had Washington family associations, it had not belonged to George Washington, nor is any tall clock documented as having been in the Mansion during Washington's lifetime. Similarly, the removal of the carpet and window hangings from the study provided new insights into Washington's practical nature and taste.

While much of the "refinement" in the Mansion has been quite subtle, it took a most dramatic form in the recent restoration of paint colors. In 1980, the Association hired Matthew Mosca, one of the country's leading experts in historic paint research, to undertake a scientific analysis of all the painted surfaces throughout the Mansion. Some 2,500 paint samples were collected and analyzed; the physical evidence was then correlated with documentary accounts. The results of his yearlong study established a complete chromochronology of the rooms dating from Washington's earliest years at Mount Vernon up to modern times. This evidence of the sequence and change of colors added significantly to the understanding of the evolution and development of the Mansion. The Mount Vernon findings also have had a major impact on the rapidly-growing body of information about painted architectural surfaces in American historic houses.

The actual restoration of the paint colors to their appearance in the last years of Washington's life took another four years to complete—working up, floor by floor, from the main floor to the garret. The first room to be affected by the new findings was Washington's study. Here, it was shown, the woodwork throughout the room was "grained," or painted to simulate wood, in this case, walnut. The plaster walls were whitewashed, the doors painted burnt-umber brown, an inexpensive and practical color that hints at the private nature of the room. The pine floors in Washington's day would have been untreated, so the floors in the study and throughout the house were stripped of accumulations of stain and wax.

The handsome and subtle restoration of the study was little preparation for the explosion of color revealed in the "public" rooms of the house. For the most part, Washington chose for these areas variations of Prussian blue and verdigris green. The samples of original paint showed that only the best quality pigments had been used, providing color of a brightness and vibrancy that startled even the experts. In the case of the verdigris green used in the small dining room, the paint was actually a translucent glaze, further enhancing the intensity of the color.

To assure the authentic appearance of the painted finishes, the original colors were not only matched, but their formulas recreated. The Mount Vernon paint crew ground the pigments by hand in oil and used specially-made round brushes of the type that would have been used in Washington's time. Where the evidence called for wallpaper, paper of the appropriate construction was applied in large sheets with slightly overlapping horizontal seams and painted to match surviving fragments of original paper.

The bright colors were set off by red mahogany graining on most of the interior doors on the first and second floors and on the paneling in the central passage.

The investigation of painted surfaces also pinpointed some architectural inaccuracies, which were corrected along the way. This included the removal of two mantels on the second and third floors, which, although of 18th-century date, were not original to the house. One of these, in the blue bedroom, was replaced with a modern reproduction scaled to match the physical evidence. The other

*The most dramatic change in the Mansion began in 1980, with a full-scale study of interior paint colors. To conform to the new findings, the pine woodwork in the study was "grained" to simulate walnut.*

mantel, in a garret room, was not replaced since there was no physical evidence that one was ever there. A more dramatic change involved the winding staircase on the third floor leading to the cupola. The staircase, which had been installed by the Army Corps of Engineers in 1869, was taken down and replaced with a simple ladder, completely changing the light and space on the third floor landing.

Based on physical and documentary evidence, a bedroom on the third floor, known to have been used by Martha Washington after her husband's death, was restored. This included the installation of a period Franklin fireplace in place of the long-lost original that had made the room habitable.

While the restoration of the interior of the Mansion continues

*After her husband's death in 1799, Martha Washington moved to this room on the third floor of the Mansion. The restoration was completed with the installation of a period Franklin fireplace in place of the missing original.*

to be refined, the preservation of the physical structure remains a top priority as time, weather and millions of visitors take their toll. In 1989, the Association hired one of the top consultant teams in the country to conduct a structural analysis of all of the historic buildings at Mount Vernon. The initial findings were re-assuring—the structural improvements made to the Mansion during the early years of the Association have withstood the passage of time, leaving George Washington's home in remarkably sound condition for its age and usage. Still, like most old homes, the Mansion has its weak points. The study highly recommended that the Association initiate a full-fledged Historic Structures Report, for the Mansion as well as the variety of historic outbuildings. When this detailed report is completed, the Association will be prepared to enter a new century armed with a master plan for the entire estate.

## OUTBUILDINGS, GARDENS AND GROUNDS

Ann Pamela Cunningham's vision of a restored Mount Vernon extended beyond the Mansion to the entire complex of outbuildings, gardens and grounds—in essence, the whole environment George Washington created. It is perhaps difficult from today's perspective to realize how revolutionary an idea this was. Though an extraordinary number of original structures survived from Washington's time, they were in dilapidated condition, a scene that must have been shocking to the prevailing Victorian sensibilities. Nevertheless, the Ladies, shunning the advice of one observer who suggested that the outbuildings be torn down because they had "housed menials," embarked on a plan of systematic repair and restoration. Writing of the urgent condition of the outbuildings, the Association's first treasurer, George Washington Riggs, expressed the guiding philosophy most succinctly: "They should I think be repaired at once, retaining in them everything that can be retained and restoring them as nearly as possible to what they were in General Washington's days."

In every era, there is a constant struggle to balance a faithfulness to the 18th-century environment against the practical necessities of running a historic house museum, given the technology and means of the times. In the early days, the Association had few options but to break some of its own rules, adapting some of the outbuildings to administrative uses, even making structural alterations in some cases. Over time, most of these adaptations have been corrected, although a few, such as the gardener's house-turned-watchroom, have been retained in order to keep the security function within the exhibition area. Restoration is ongoing as research and archaeology continue to

85

uncover new information about existing structures and those no longer standing.

While many of the outbuildings have been extensively repaired (some to the point where there is very little "original" fabric left), there are only two structures that are true reconstructions. The coach house on the south lane was reconstructed in 1893–94. A more major project was the reconstruction of the greenhouse-slave quarters complex, which was completed in 1952, just before the Association's centennial. It is a good example of a project that was appropriately delayed until the technology, scholarship and financing were right.

Located on the north side of the upper garden, the stately brick greenhouse with its flanking slave quarter wings was Washington's last major addition to the Mansion House Farm before his death. Its innovative design included underground flues that channeled heat but not smoke from the slave quarter fireplaces on the north side to the central greenhouse on the south. This complex system, however, may have been the cause of the fire that destroyed the building on a bitter winter night in 1835, making it one of the few structures standing in 1799 that had not survived when the Association acquired the property in 1858.

In the earliest years of the Association's ownership, a small "modern" greenhouse was built over the ruins of the original, and the sale of seeds and cuttings became an important source of income. Somewhat later, the slave quarter wings were rebuilt and adapted as lodging for members of the Association during the annual Council meetings. The rebuilt structures were recognized as an intrusion on Washington's plan, but lack of documentation about the original buildings, limited funds and other circumstances delayed serious consideration of an authentic reconstruction until well into the 20th century.

In the 1930s, bolstered by increasing attendance and advances in the relatively new field of historical archaeaology, the Association launched an extensive examination of the outbuildings and grounds. As the major structure missing from the original layout, the greenhouse-slave quarters received particular attention. By 1935, sufficient evidence had been gathered to draw up a plan for a reconstruction of the original building, yet the problem of displacing the Vice Regents who still occupied rooms in the slave quarter wings prevented immediate action. While plans were made to construct new Vice Regents' quarters on the north end of the property, well away from the exhibition area, the project was further delayed by World War II and the resulting cutbacks.

It was not until the early 1950s that the Association was finally in a position to move ahead, breaking ground for the new Vice Regents' quarters as the 19th-century greenhouse, now with many appendages, was torn down. Demolition allowed a more complete archaeological examination confirming that much of the original wall footings had been incorporated into the later structures. Added to the physical evidence were specifications found in Washington's correspondence and the critical discovery of two early 19th-century insurance policies that included renderings of the greenhouse facade. A timely contribution to the project came from the Commission on Renovation of the Executive Mansion, which donated a large quan-

*In the early 1950s, the Association reconstructed the last major structure missing from the 1799 layout of the estate. Washington's original greenhouse/slave quarters, on the north side of the upper garden, had burned in 1835, and over a century passed before sufficient documentary and physical evidence made possible an accurate reconstruction.*

tity of handmade 18th-century brick that had been displaced during the Truman administration's renovation of the White House.

Although a modern heating system was installed, the greenhouse functions again as it did in Washington's day, housing the potted and tubbed "exotics" such as hibiscus, oleander, palm and citrus trees, which are moved out onto the garden courtyard according to the season.

The Association went on to refurnish and put on public view several rooms in the slave quarters, including a shoemaker's shop in the rear of the greenhouse, mentioned in one of Washington's letters to his manager. Also on view is a dormitory-style living area, furnished with built-in bunk beds or "berths" as interpreted from documentary evidence. Other sections of the wings have been given adaptive use, including a small museum shop on the west end and an area for special exhibitions on the east. Because it is a reconstructed structure, fires are allowed to burn in a slave quarter fireplace, providing the evocative smell of woodsmoke that would have predominated the grounds in the 18th century.

Mount Vernon was the first historic house museum in America to actively preserve buildings relating to slave life, first stabilizing and repairing them in the 19th century, and eventually restoring and refurnishing them according to period documentation. Plantation life in all its aspects remains a central theme for the ongoing research and archaeological programs, as the key to a clearer understanding of the complex community of people, white and black, who lived and worked at Mount Vernon.

Archaeological excavations have been a critical part of the restoration process since the 1930s. In 1985, the Association established a full-fledged Department of Archaeology to pull together and analyze the findings of the past, as well as to begin a systematic and ongoing study of the evolution of the entire estate, above and below ground.

Among the Department of Archaeology's first investigations was a comprehensive look at evidence of Washington's blacksmith shop on the north lane and the long-standing debate over whether it was still in existence in 1799. A small brick structure known to have been used originally as an ice house stands on a portion of the original blacksmith shop site, which has been much disturbed over the years by construction and the installation of utility lines. Nevertheless, excavations have recovered extensive evidence of the blacksmithing operation, including structural remains of the shop itself and associated fence lines, as well as iron and iron waste, fragments of brass, black ashy soils and large quantities of slag, coal and charcoal. The site is currently marked with an interpretive sign, showing a hypothetical perspective view of the blacksmith shop and surrounding yards, based on the archaeological and documentary evidence.

Like the outbuildings, the restoration of the gardens and grounds has evolved over the years as time, technology and scholarship have allowed a more thorough look at the surviving evidence of their appearance in 1799. In 1980, the botanical garden, where Washington experimented with rare and unusual plants and seeds, was replanted with the species known to have been grown there. More recently, a dramatic transformation has taken place in the upper garden, as the result of several years of intensive research.

While the location and shape of the upper garden were well established by the surviving outer walls, the interior layout had undergone many changes over the generations, obscuring much of the original configuration. Research showed that the elaborate rose beds on either side of the main walkway had been added in the 19th century. These were removed and replaced with simpler square and rectangular beds, planted with a profusion of flowers, herbs, fruit trees and, in one section, vegetables, according to period documentation. The roses were interspersed throughout the garden in a manner more typical of the 18th century. A final step in the restoration was the extension of the outer walk around the perimeter of

89

the garden, requiring an alteration and replanting of the fleur-de-lis pattern of boxwood in the east parterre.

Only varieties of plants known to have been available in Washington's time are grown in the garden beds. The prized feature of the upper garden is the boxwood that survives from a 1798 planting, a critical clue to the original layout of the walks and beds.

In practice, Washington was both an avid horticulturist and a landscape architect, although he would have simply called himself a gentleman farmer. He was a follower of the English school of naturalistic landscape design, adapting its principles to his own needs in the near-wilderness setting of Mount Vernon. He took full advantage of the sweeping panorama of the Potomac River and Maryland shoreline to the east of the Mansion. Below the east lawn, in the deer park on the slope that leads to the river, Washington cultivated a "hanging wood" of flowering trees and shrubs kept low to set off the view. The restoration of this important element of the landscape has been funded by a gift in honor of Rose Forsyth Strachan, Vice Regent Emeritus for Louisiana and, for many years, Chairman of the Gardens and Grounds Committee.

Attention has also been focused on the area between the tomb and the stable known as the "vineyard enclosure." Although the cultivation of grapes was generally unsuccessful, the area was also used for the propagation of nursery stock and fruit trees. Horticultural research has identified the many varieties of plants and trees that were grown there, while archaeological investigations are under way to determine the original fence lines and arrangement of the plantings.

*The restoration of the upper garden recreated the formal pleasure garden established by George Washington. Boxwood planted in 1798 lines the garden walks, and flowers and plants from the period are grown in the garden beds.*

*In his last will and testament, George Washington specified the location for a new family enclosure. but the new tomb was not completed until almost 40 years after his death. The obelisks on either side of the tomb are memorials to the 19th-century Washington family members who owned Mount Vernon.*

## THE TOMB

As visitors walk down the south lane from the Mansion and turn the corner toward Washington's tomb, they leave the 18th-century environment and enter a timeless one. Although Washington had chosenthe site and planned the simple brick structure, the "new tomb," as it is called, was not completed until 1837. In the 19th century, the tomb was the focus for the visitors who came to pay homage to the father of his country; in fact, the case might be made that it is because of the tomb that Mount Vernon was saved at all.

For many, the tomb remains a place to reflect on the greatness of Washington's character, without being diverted by the fascinating details of an 18th-century home and plantation. Of all areas at Mount Vernon, the solemn and peaceful setting around Washington's tomb is perhaps the least changed over time.

One very subtle addition took nearly 90 years to accomplish and has an interesting story behind it. In the courtyard in front of the tomb stand two marble obelisks that were erected by the Washington family in 1850 to commemorate the 19th-century owners of Mount Vernon who are interred in the family vault. One was inscribed with the name of Bushrod Washington (1762–1829) and his wife, Ann Blackburn; the other with John Augustine Washington (1789–1832), whose wife, Jane Charlotte Blackburn, was still living at the time.

When John Augustine Washington, Jr., finally negotiated the sale of 200 acres of Mount Vernon to Miss Cunningham and her Ladies, the agreement specified that the Washington family would retain the rights to one quarter-acre square surrounding Washington's tomb. They also agreed that there would be no further burials within the vault; as tradition has it, the key was thrown into the river.

In 1894, Jean Charlotte Washington Yeatman, a relative of the last private owner, approached the Association through her Daughters of the American Revolution chapter for permission to have inscribed on John Augustine Washington's obelisk the name of his wife, Jane Charlotte, and son, John Augustine Washington, Jr., to complete the history of family ownership. According to the minutes of the Council meeting, the Association "courteously declined" to grant permission to the DAR, but did rule that Mrs. Yeatman, as a member of the family, would have the privilege of adding an inscription. The name of Jane Charlotte Blackburn Washington, who was entombed within the family vault in 1855, was finally added in 1910.

It was not until 1981 that descendants of the last private owner reopened the issue, requesting again that the names of John Augustine Washington, Jr., and his wife, Eleanor Love Selden, be inscribed on his father's monument. Although the 19th-century minutes were discreetly silent about the details, modern-day staff members were able to piece together evidence suggesting that the project was halted because of disagreement over the family's request to include on the inscription John A. Washington's military rank in the Army of the Confederate States of America. The opposition was most likely led by the staunch Unionist, Miss Alice Longfellow, daughter of the poet and Vice Regent for Massachusetts.

A fascinated Council reheard the case and quickly consented to grant permission for the additional inscription. Although John A. Washington and his wife both died after they left Mount Vernon and are buried side by side at Zion Episcopal Church in Charles Town, West Virginia, it was decided that they should rightfully be commemorated with their predecessors as owners and protectors of Mount Vernon.

In August 1983, several of their descendants gathered for the unveiling of the new inscription, which reads:

In memory

of

JOHN AUGUSTINE WASHINGTON

LT. COL., C.S.A.

1820–1861

and his wife

ELEANOR LOVE SELDEN

1824–1860

Last private owners of Mount Vernon

Buried at Charles Town, West Virginia

South of Washington's tomb, on a high wooded bluff overlooking the river, lies an area identified as a burial ground for slaves and free blacks who lived and worked at Mount Vernon in the 18th and 19th centuries. In 1929, under the leadership of the Vice Regent for Texas, Mrs. Thomas S. Maxey, the Association erected a simple marble monument to mark the site. A new memorial to those who served in slavery at Mount Vernon, planned in cooperation with members of the local black community, was dedicated in 1983. Designed by a team of students from the Howard University School of Architecture, the new memorial features a truncated column surrounded by a circular brick courtyard, providing a place for quiet contemplation. Around the base of the column in bronze letters are the words HOPE, FAITH, and LOVE.

## BEYOND THE EXHIBITION AREA

The preservation of Mount Vernon extends well beyond the roughly 30 acres that make up the area on exhibition to the public. Just as Washington negotiated land deals with his neighbors to build his estate piece by piece, the Association over the years has more than doubled its original 200 acres through gifts and the purchase of adjacent tracts. Today the Association owns about 500 acres of land, approximating the boundaries of George Washington's Mansion House Farm. Heeding Miss Cunningham's warning against the "fingers of progress," the Association has created its own "buffer zone" to protect the historic area from the sights and sounds of the modern world.

The ultimate challenge to Miss Cunningham's vision of a Mount Vernon saved from change began in the 1950s, when the Association was first confronted by the threat of modern development across the river. Since Washington's time, the most consistently remarked upon feature of the estate in visitors' accounts was the magnificent view from the piazza across the broad Potomac River to the hills and fields of Maryland. This pastoral scene is an essential part of Washington's landscape design, stretching as far as the eye can see and certainly far beyond the boundaries of the Association's property. Faced with the spread of postwar suburban development on both sides of the river, the Ladies found themselves forging again into uncharted territory in the field of historic preservation.

Up until that time the Association might have been described as decidedly isolationist. After their initial fund-raising campaign, the Ladies turned inward, focusing their energies on the restoration

95

and maintenance of the property they held in trust for the nation. They took great pride in their self-sufficiency, deflecting publicity about themselves while constantly working behind the scenes to promote the memory of George Washington. Their single-mindedness and independence had been the key to their success. The threat to the overview, however, called for new tactics, and in the course of its struggle the Association would seek the help and support of private citizens, community organizations, state agencies and, finally, the federal government.

Across the river in Maryland, local residents were also organizing to protect the rural nature of their area, forming a community league called the Moyaone Association, named for an early Indian village. Adding strength to their cause was the Alice Ferguson Foundation, created from the estate of one of their members to promote the conservation and educational use of the land.

The crisis that brought the two sides together occurred when an oil refining company opened negotiations to buy a large tract of land directly across from Mount Vernon to use as an oil tank farm. Though deeply alarmed, the Ladies initially were reluctant to get directly involved in an area out of their legal jurisdiction as a Virginia corporation. Then, one of their own members, Frances Payne Bolton, the Vice Regent for Ohio and a member of Congress, stepped in with her own funds and purchased the threatened 485-acre tract known as Bryan Point.

Inspired by her generosity and vision, the Association fully embraced the cause and joined forces with its Maryland neighbors and the National Park Service to form the Accokeek Foundation, Inc., the purpose of which is to protect and preserve the natural beauty of the land opposite Mount Vernon and foster its use for educational and scientific purposes. Mrs. Bolton was elected first president of

*Due to the efforts of Frances Payne Bolton, the Association's Vice Regent for Ohio from 1938 to 1977 and a member of Congress, the view from Mount Vernon across the Potomac River remains much the same as it was 200 years ago.*

the foundation. Through her leadership and political expertise, the foundation created a national board that showed keen sensitivity to the interests of the local community. The Bryan Point property, along with several hundred additional acres purchased by Mrs. Bolton, became the nucleus of the foundation's efforts to acquire river-front property, establish scenic easements and promote restrictive building covenants to protect a six-mile stretch along the Maryland shore.

The Accokeek Foundation continued as a solely private initiative until 1960, when the Washington Suburban Sanitary Commission, exercising its legislated power of eminent domain, decided to build a sewage treatment plant on Mockley Point facing Mount Vernon, because, as they said, "there is nothing there." When the state of Maryland could do nothing to intervene, the Accokeek Foundation finally turned to the federal government with a proposal that a National Park be created to protect the land once and for all.

Late in 1961, after a considerable lobbying effort by the Accokeek Foundation and its supporters, Congress passed Public Law 87-362, which authorized the National Park Service to accept donations of land from the Accokeek Foundation and the Alice Ferguson Foundation, to purchase certain adjacent lands and to establish scenic easements to create Piscataway National Park. It was a unique type of federal park, whose administration would continue to work closely with the Accokeek Foundation board to assure the protection of the Mount Vernon overview.

While the Association celebrated this victory, the struggle was not over. The bill that passed was only enabling legislation; the necessary funds to carry it out had not been appropriated. The next 13 years saw a frustrating series of Congressional budgetary requests eliminated in the House, reappropriated in the Senate and compromised in conference, as soaring land costs drove up the amount needed year by year. Finally in 1974, President Gerald Ford signed into law a bill that provided funds to complete Piscataway National Park, now a 4000-acre preserve of federal and private land. Its centerpiece is the National Colonial Farm, a living history museum of colonial agriculture.

The Mount Vernon Ladies' Association continues as an active member and financial supporter of the Accokeek Foundation, which remains ever alert to possible encroachments beyond the protected area. Most recently, the Association hired the Trust for Public Land to evaluate the entire region within Mount Vernon's "viewshed," in a far-reaching commitment to preservation in its truest sense.

The preservation effort extends upward as well. In 1968, after years of persistent requests from the Association, the Federal Aviation Administration decreed an area 1,500 feet over Mount Vernon as restricted from all types of air traffic, providing at least a measure of protection from noise pollution and the chance of a serious air accident.

## COLLECTIONS AND SCHOLARSHIP

At the end of the north lane, to the east of the greenhouse-quarters complex, is a small museum built in 1928 for the display of Washington "relics" that could not be shown to best advantage in the room settings of the Mansion. Although the building was designed to blend in with the clapboard, shingled-roof style of the outbuildings, it does not represent an original structure. Within this unassuming but highly protected space, the visitor can view at close range some of the Association's greatest treasures.

Most valued among these possessions is the original terra cotta bust of George Washington, which was modeled at Mount Vernon by the French sculptor Jean Antoine Houdon in 1785. It is considered the best likeness of Washington.

Also on display in the Museum is Samuel Vaughan's 1787 plan of Mount Vernon, the earliest known delineation of Washington's formal grounds and a document of critical importance to the restoration of the estate. On loan to the Association since the 1940s, the Vaughan plan was purchased from descendants of Martha Washington in 1976. Samuel Vaughan's journal containing notes about his visit to Mount Vernon and the original sketch for the larger plan was presented to Mount Vernon through the generosity of several of his descendants in 1989.

Among other outstanding recent accessions is a collection of 34 pieces of Washington and Custis silver, presented in 1982 by Mrs. A. Smith Bowman and Robert E. Lee IV, descendants of Martha Washington. Their father, Dr. George Bolling Lee, had originally placed this superb family collection on loan to the Association in 1936, at which time a special museum case was prepared for its display. Another collection of Washington/Custis memorabilia, lent anonymously in 1980, included several additional pieces of silver as well as porcelain, textiles and glassware. The Association's Annual Reports over the last decades provide a chronicle of the steady return of original Washington and Custis memorabilia through gift, purchase and loan.

Mount Vernon is unique among historic house museums for the size and scope of its library collections. While the Association began acquiring original Washington books and manuscripts in the 19th century, a separate library department was not established until 1937.

Since that time there has been a major effort to seek out and acquire documentary material relating to the history of Mount Vernon and the lives of its principal residents. The historical manuscript col-

*A layout of the estate drawn by Samuel Vaughan in 1787 after a visit to Mount Vernon has proved to be an invaluable tool in the restoration of the outbuildings and grounds. The Association also owns Vaughan's original journal, containing notes about his visit to Mount Vernon.*

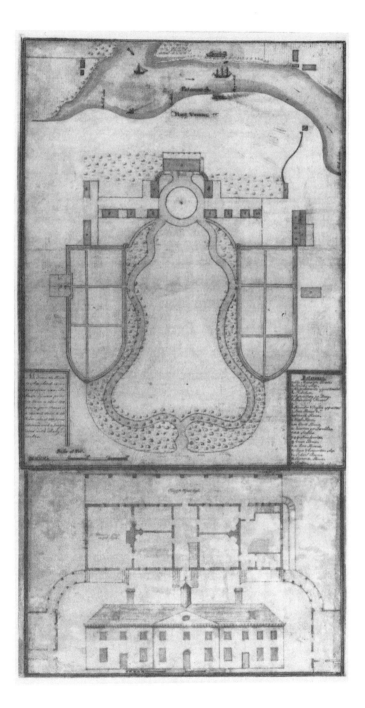

lection contains over 5,000 original Washington family papers, from an English land deed on vellum dated 1601 to the correspondence of the last private owner, John Augustine Washington, Jr., and his children. Included in this collection are over 500 original George Washington letters, ledgers, account books, surveys and an original diary, as well as the largest single collection of the letters of Martha Washington, numbering over 40. The library also houses the extensive Association archives, documenting in rich detail the history of the nation's first historic preservation movement.

In an effort to recreate Washington's personal library, the Association has acquired over 80 original volumes, along with a growing collection of duplicate editions of titles he is known to have owned. The reference library collection, now approximately 10,000 volumes, focuses on George Washington and his contemporaries, 18th-century plantation life, decorative arts, historic preservation and other related fields of study. Since 1984, most of the reference library acquisitions have been funded from an endowment established by the William Randolph Hearst Foundation in honor of Phoebe Apperson Hearst, who served as Vice Regent for California from 1889 to 1918. Two similar endowments were created by the Flagler Foundation and a member of the Mount Vernon Advisory Committee, Lawrence Lewis; and in honor of C. Waller Barrett, a long-time advisor to Mount Vernon and one of America's premier collectors of rare books.

While the Association remains active in the competitive and ever-escalating manuscript and rare book market, the collections have been greatly enhanced by several major gifts from Washington family descendants and private collectors.

The earliest of these gifts was also one of the most important. In 1944, Mrs. DeCourcy Thom, Vice Regent for Maryland and a Washington family descendant, donated a collection of over 100 manuscripts from George Washington's personal archives. Among the papers were 45 previously-unknown letters written by Lund Washington, George Washington's cousin and manager of Mount Vernon in Washington's absence during the Revolutionary War.

Also in the collection are several weekly work reports of the Mount Vernon gardeners, spinners and carpenters, and correspondence concerning the purchase of goods and services through Washington's Philadelphia agent, Clement Biddle.

In 1976, Dr. Sol Feinstone presented an extraordinary collection of 127 letters written by George Washington to William

*George Washington purchased this four-volume set of* The Life and Adventures of the Renowned Don Quixote *in Philadelphia on September 17, 1787, the same day that the Constitution was adopted. The volumes, each containing Washington's distinctive signature on the title page, were returned to Mount Vernon in 1983 through the generosity of the William Randolph Hearst Foundation.*

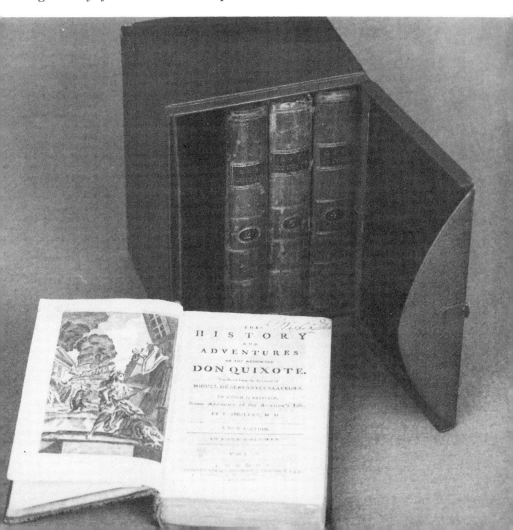

Pearce, who managed Mount Vernon during Washington's second presidential term. These papers provide not only an almost weekly account of work being done at Mount Vernon during the mid-1790s, but also clearly show Washington's detailed involvement in almost every aspect of the estate's management, even in his absence.

The signed indenture by which 22-year-old George Washington leased Mount Vernon from his half brother's widow in 1754 was purchased in 1985 through a grant from the Kohler Company of Wisconsin. This landmark document signaled the beginning of Washington's 45-year tenure as proprietor of Mount Vernon. The collection now includes almost all of the major land title papers that trace the succession of the estate through the Washington family from the original patent granted to Washington's great-grandfather in 1674.

In recent years the Association has also received three major collections that offer a broad survey of Washington iconography in the 18th and 19th centuries. In 1984, Mr. and Mrs. Robert B. Gibby presented the Willard-Budd collection of 200 historical prints relating to events in Washington's life. Mr. Gibby was also the moving force behind the production of an educational videotape, *The Life of George Washington*, illustrated with selections from the collection he assembled. The Stanley D. Scott Collection of printed and medallic portraits of George Washington, presented in 1985, includes several hundred engravings, lithographs, badges, coins and medals, bringing together some of the finest and rarest examples of popular Washington portraiture. Dr. and Mrs. Joseph Fields have donated several important examples from their extensive collection of Washington images, as well as an outstanding collection of eulogies and orations on the death of George Washington.

The library collections are used extensively by the staff to support the ongoing research and restoration of Mount Vernon. The li-

*One of the most significant manuscripts in the Mount Vernon Library Collection is the original lease to the estate, signed by George Washington in 1754. Added to the collection in 1985, the document marks the beginning of Washington's 45-year tenure at Mount Vernon.*

brary is also open to outside readers by appointment. In a commodious new facility that opened in 1983, scholars have a unique opportunity to study Washington within steps of the environment he created.

One of the most enduring contributions to the field of Washington scholarship is the Association's co-sponsorship with the University of Virginia of a new comprehensive edition of *The Papers of George Washington*. Since the inception of the project in 1968, the Association has provided financial support, encouragement and scholarly assistance to the editorial staff based in Charlottesville, Virginia. The project also receives a grant from the National Endowment for the Humanities to match the Association's annual contribution and gifts from other sources.

There was good precedent for the Association's involvement in such a far-reaching, scholarly undertaking. In the 1920s, the Ladies commissioned Dr. John C. Fitzpatrick to edit the first published edition of the diaries of George Washington, which came out in four volumes. Dr. Fitzpatrick went on to become editor of the 39-volume *Writings of George Washington*, published between 1931 and 1940, as part of the federal government's celebration of the 200th anniversary of George Washington's birth. The Fitzpatrick edition superseded two much-more-limited 19th-century editions of Washington's writings and opened the way to a great flowering of Washington scholarship, most notably Douglas Southall Freeman's monumental seven-volume biography. The availability of the Fitzpatrick editions of Washington's writings and diaries also allowed the Association to make great strides with its own research and restoration programs.

As unpublished Washington documents have come to light over the decades, Fitzpatrick's edition has been rendered incomplete. As was the case with the earlier editors, he did not include letters written to George Washington, which are essential to a full understanding of the papers. The approach of the nation's bicentennial underscored the need for a new, and for the first time, comprehensive edition of Washington's papers. The Association took on co-sponsorship of *The Papers of George Washington* as its major contribution to the bicentennial celebration.

Since the project began the editors of *The Papers of George Washington* have gathered more than 135,000 individual items, and previously unknown material continues to surface. The completed series is projected to run upward of 85 volumes. First issued was a new, extensively-annotated edition of Washington's diaries complete in six volumes, which were published between 1976 and 1980. These were followed by the publication in one volume of *The Journal of the Proceedings of the President, 1793–1797*, an adjunct to the diaries that provides a record of Washington's actions as chief executive of the new nation. Washington's correspondence and other papers are now being published simultaneously in four series, Colonial, Revolutionary War, Confederation and Presidential, in a much-heralded plan to give scholars earlier access to important material from later periods of Washington's life. The new edition of *The Papers of George Washington* will provide the fundamental resources for all future Washington scholarship; its impact is already being felt in the ongoing research and restoration programs at Mount Vernon.

## Growth and Development

The annual attendance figures are one of the best barometers of the times at Mount Vernon, the visiting public being the Association's principal source of support. From the time the Association first opened its doors to visitors in 1858, charging 25 cents admission, attendance rose slowly and fairly steadily from a few thousand a year to a high of 856,941 on the eve of World War II. In 1944, the number of annual visitors dropped to under 175,000 as the nation was diverted by the war effort. During this time, the Association had to make major cutbacks in its staff and restoration programs to assure basic maintenance of the estate.

After the war, attendance quickly increased, reflecting the booming economy and a renewed interest in the nation's historical roots. In 1952, on the eve of the Association's centennial, the number of annual visitors reached the one million mark. During the following decades, attendance has averaged about 1,100,000 a year, rarely fluctuating more than 10 percent. "Fair weather and the New York World's Fair" are credited with bringing the record number of annual visitors, 1,347,742, in 1964. In 1974, the nation's gas shortage caused attendance to dip below one million for the first time in 23 years.

In the field of historic house museums, Mount Vernon ranks second only to the White House in number of annual visitors. However, the leveling off of attendance rates began to put a strain on the Association's financial resources as inflation and escalating operating costs took their toll. Admission fees were gradually increased over the years, but only in compliance with the Association's commitment to keeping a visit to Mount Vernon within the means of the average American family. By the late 1970s, it was clear that the Association could not continue to rely on gate receipts and a few private donations to cover both its operating budget and a growing list of needed capital improvements.

In 1980, the Association launched a nationwide capital campaign, the first since Ann Pamela Cunningham's initial effort to raise funds to purchase the estate in the 1850s. The goal was set at $10 million; by January 1985, when the campaign officially closed, more than $11 million had been raised from corporate, foundation and individual donors. As their predecessors had done in the 19th century, the Vice Regents championed the cause in their individual states and reached their goal in only five years.

The campaign touched nearly every aspect of the Mount Vernon operation. One of the most visible achievements was the construction of the Ann Pamela Cunningham Building, a long-needed research and administrative center adjacent to the exhibition area. The project began with the erection of an electronic security gate on the north end of the property that literally "opened the way" for heavy construction vehicles to have access to the building site. Funded by the William Randolph Hearst Foundation and named in honor of Phoebe Apperson Hearst, the gate provides a secured entrance to the administrative areas without disrupting the historic environment.

The Ann Pamela Cunningham Building houses the Association's extensive library, archival and curatorial study collections in secure, climate-controlled storage areas. It also features a spacious library reading room, conservation laboratory, exhibition hall and meeting rooms, as well as staff offices. Dedicated in 1983, the new building has greatly facilitated the research activities of the staff and outside scholars and has attracted a number of important gifts to the collections.

The old administration building, which was originally built as Vice Regents' quarters, was renovated to provide additional office space and areas for meetings and receptions. It was renamed in honor of Frances Payne Bolton, Vice Regent for Ohio from 1938 to 1977, in recognition of her many contributions to the preservation of Mount Vernon and Washington's view across the river.

Since Washington's time, the threat of fire has been the greatest concern of Mount Vernon's proprietors, as generation after generation have applied the best of the prevailing technology toward fire prevention. "There is nothing that fills my mind with more apprehension when I am from home than Fire," Washington wrote to his manager in 1791, requesting that every precaution be taken to guard against the danger of fire. As part of the capital campaign, the fire detection and suppression systems throughout the estate were completely renovated, including the innovative installation of ionization detectors backed by Halon 1301 gas in the Mansion. This specially-designed system is virtually invisible to the visiting public and was installed with minimal disturbance to the historic fabric of the building. In 1981, the Ford Motor Company Fund donated a new fire engine that replaced one that had been given by Henry Ford himself in 1936.

The campaign also raised funds to support the upgrading and modernization of the electrical and security systems in the Mansion and throughout the estate. The underground irrigation sys-

*In the reading room of the Ann Pamela Cunningham Building, above, staff and outside scholars can study original manuscripts and reference books from the Mount Vernon library collections. The Ann Pamela Cunningham Building, left, a research and administrative center, was the most visible result of the capital development campaign launched by the Association in 1980.*

tem for the gardens and grounds was improved and extended. In 1986, a new production greenhouse complex was dedicated, expanding the Association's capabilities in plant production and horticultural research.

*In 1899, when a new entrance gate to the estate was required, the Vice Regent for Texas, Mrs. Thomas S. Maxey, collected funds from the schoolchildren and Masons of Texas to build the "Texas Gate." Nearly 90 years later, when the Texas Gate required repairs and modernization, the current Vice Regent for Texas, Mrs. Thomas Dunaway Anderson, raised more than $350,000 for a complete renovation of the gate.*

While many of the campaign projects strengthened Mount Vernon "behind the scenes," a most visible accomplishment was the renovation of the historic "Texas Gate," the main entrance for the general public. The gate was constructed in 1899 to accommodate the then-hundreds of visitors who arrived by carriage or on the new trolley line. Mrs. Thomas S. Maxey, then Vice Regent for Texas, had collected nickels and dimes from schoolchildren across her state and enlisted the support of the Texas Masons to raise funds to build the original gate. Almost 90 years later, Texans again took up the cause. Under the leadership of Mrs. Thomas Dunaway Anderson, Vice Regent for Texas, more than $350,000 was raised from the Lone Star State for the Texas Gate project, principally through the participation of the Grand Lodge of Texas. The renovations preserve the architectural grace of the original structure, while adding computerized ticketing equipment and additional security.

The most important and forward-looking achievement of the capital campaign was the establishment of an endowment that will provide a more secure fiscal foundation while allowing the Association to keep entrance fees at a modest level. The endowment also supports the acquisition of original Washington memorabilia, books and manuscripts.

Building upon the renewed public interest in Mount Vernon generated by the capital campaign, the Association in 1985 initiated its first annual support programs—Friends of Historic Mount Vernon and the Mount Vernon One Hundred. Membership privileges include merchandise discounts, special programs and a subscription to the Association's newsletter, *Yesterday, Today, Tomorrow*. A group called the Neighborhood Friends of Historic Mount Vernon was also formed, whose members all live on property that was originally part of George Washington's 8,000-acre estate.

During this period of growth and development, the Association also expanded its operation to assume management of the Mount Vernon Inn, a National Park Service concession located just outside the Texas Gate. A new corporate subsidiary, Mount Vernon Inn, Inc., was created in 1981. Since that time, major renovations have been made in the restaurant, snack bar and gift shop areas, assuring that these important visitor services are in keeping with the total Mount Vernon experience. The Museum Shop, located within the historic area, has also been carefully redesigned to offer an expanded inventory of gift items and publications relating to the Washingtons and plantation life. Combining marketing and educational purposes, the Association has launched a selective program to create authorized museum reproductions and related products, issued under its own trademark.

## PUBLIC OUTREACH

In planning its programs, the Association's first responsibility is to the individual visitor who pays his or her admission and tours the estate. The visitor may arrive by car, bus, boat or bicycle; alone or with family, on a group tour or school field trip. The visitor may have just an hour to see the Mansion and grounds, or the person may be able to spend the entire day. If the visitor arrives during the busy season (April through October), he or she may be one of 8,000 or more who visit Mount Vernon in a given day.

It is for this visitor that the general interpretive program is designed. The essentially self-guided tour of the estate is enhanced by on-site interpreters, informative signs, exhibits, brochures and other publications. Basic to the Association's philosophy is the belief that the faithfully-restored site is the best reflection of Washington's character. The interpretation of Mount Vernon is designed to allow individual visitors to discover Washington for themselves.

A principal part of the Association's mission, as stated in its original charter of 1858, is "to perpetuate the memory of the Father of his Country." While this is most effectively done within the Mount Vernon environment, the charge also challenges the Association to reach out to people who may never have a chance to visit the estate. Since the days of the *Mount Vernon Record*, a journal that was published from 1856 to 1858 and included articles on George Washington's life and character, the Association has sought to bring its message to a national audience.

The Association has sponsored and produced a number of publications on a wide range of subjects relating to George Washington and Mount Vernon. The much-admired Mount Vernon Handbook has been revised and expanded over the years to reflect ongoing developments in research and restoration. Specialized publications have focused on the gardens and grounds, music and decorative arts. Charles C. Wall's *George Washington: Citizen-Soldier* offers a unique perspective on Washington's public and private life during the American Revolution. *The Mount Vernon Cookbook*, sponsored by The Founders, Washington Committee for Historic Mount Vernon, combines modern receipts with a historical introduction about food preparation at Mount Vernon in the 18th century. Recently, donors from the state of Michigan supported a revised edition of John Frederick Schroeder's *Maxims of George Washington*, a compendium of selections from Washington's writings that was originally published in 1854. Also published was a new annotated edition of *George Washington's Rules of Civility & Decent Behaviour in Company and Conversation*, taken from a youthful Washington's school exercise book, with an introduction by the well-known etiquette expert Letitia Baldrige.

To meet the demands of a new generation, the Association has branched out into videotapes. *Mount Vernon: The Home of George Washington* presents a detailed tour of Washington's plantation, and *The Life of George Washington* offers a biographical narrative illustrated with historical prints from the Willard-Budd Collection.

School-age children are a significant part of the Mount Vernon audience, counting for about one third of the annual number of visitors. In recent years, as part of its expanded educational programs, the Association has offered special guided tours during the less-crowded winter months for grade school classes, supplemented by a pre-visit teacher's guide.

To reach children who many never have the opportunity to visit Mount Vernon, and to further enhance the understanding of those who will, the Mount Vernon education department developed a special George Washington lesson to be used within the classroom. A pilot program was launched in the state of Virginia during the 1988–89 academic year. Every fourth and fifth grade class in the public and private schools throughout the state received a special lesson package, developed by the education department in cooperation with teachers and other educational specialists.

The lesson emphasizes the qualities of Washington's character—his hard work, integrity and leadership—that were indispensable to the founding of the nation. The teacher's manual includes a biography of Washington written at the fourth and fifth grade level, and a lesson plan that further explores the ideas and values exemplified by Washington's life. To provide immediate reinforcement, students can test their knowledge on a "scratch and learn" card of questions and answers. The lesson also encourages participation in an Association-sponsored essay contest.

The first year was extraordinarily successful for a program introduced from outside the school systems—approximately 78,000 students, or nearly half of the fourth and fifth graders in Virginia, participated in the lesson. The following year, the program was also offered to the fifth graders of Kentucky, Maryland and Mississippi. The Association continues to seek state-by-state funding to bring the George Washington lesson to schoolchildren across the nation.

Another youth-oriented program is the Historic Trail for Boy Scouts, Girl Scouts and Campfire Clubs, also inaugurated in 1989. Through a series of on-site explorations and readings, members of these organizations may earn points toward a special Mount Vernon badge. During wintertime "Scouting Months," scouts in uniform are admitted to the estate free of charge.

The bicentennial of the founding of the nation refocused attention on George Washington and Mount Vernon. The Association had a major part in the nation's commemoration of events that began with the signing of the Declaration of Independence in 1776 and culminated in Washington's inauguration as the first President of the United States of America in 1789.

In 1976, France presented as its bicentennial gift to the American people a *son et lumiere* dramatization for Mount Vernon entitled "The Father of Liberty." President Gerald Ford and French President Valery Giscard d'Estaing attended the sound and light program's premiere in May of that year. More than 100,000 people attended the show over two summer seasons.

Washington's indispensable role in the creation of the nation continued as a theme in the Association's programs throughout the bicentennial period. The Association sponsored a number of special events, including lectures, seminars, exhibitions, and public ceremonies to mark specific historic anniversaries. In 1982, the celebration of the 250th anniversary of George Washington's birth further emphasized Washington's character and his rise from relatively humble beginnings to become America's greatest hero. The Association lent objects from its collections to major exhibitions at the Smithsonian's National Museum of American History, the National Portrait Gallery and the Alderman Library of the University of Virginia. President Ronald Reagan laid a wreath at Washington's tomb on February 22 and from the west door of the Mansion delivered a nationally-broadcast address to the schoolchildren of America.

Historians cite the Mount Vernon Conference of 1785 as the beginning of the movement that produced the United States Constitution. At this historic meeting, commissioners from Virginia and Maryland gathered at Mount Vernon to discuss navigational rights on the states' common waterways. It was the first example of organized interstate cooperation that led to the 1787 Constitutional Convention in Philadelphia. Among the events marking this historic anniversary in 1985 was a scholarly conference entitled "The Constitution: Commerce and the Pursuit of Happiness," co-sponsored by the Association and Project '87, a joint effort of the American History Association and the American Political Science Association.

*In a ceremony cosponsored by the Association and the Commission on the Bicentennial of the U.S. Constitution, "George Washington" and his traveling companions leave Mount Vernon on the first leg of their journey to New York, recreating Washington's journey to his inauguration in April 1789.*

An exhibit entitled "The Call of His Country: George Washington and the Constitution," featuring books, manuscripts and objects from the Mount Vernon collections, was mounted in the Museum. In June of 1988, a replica of the Federalist, a miniature sailing vessel that was presented by the citizens of Maryland to George Washington, was sailed to Mount Vernon in a reenactment of the original voyage.

The bicentennial observances culminated in a full-scale reenactment of George Washington's journey from Mount Vernon to New York City for his inauguration. The Association played a major role in the planning of this multi-state event, which was coordinated by the Commission on the Bicentennial of the United States Constitution. The reenactment of the 250-mile inaugural journey began at Mount Vernon on April 16, 1989, when actors portraying Washington and his traveling companions departed Mount Vernon by carriage during a public ceremony attended by thousands of visitors.

Bicentennial celebrations were not limited to the United States. At the request of the American Embassy in Paris, the Association agreed to lend the key to the Bastille to the government of France in July 1989 for their celebration of the 200th anniversary of Bastille Day and the French Revolution. The Regent, Mrs. Robert Channing Seamans, Jr., personally presented the historic key to French President Francois Mitterrand as President George Bush looked on. The carefully-guarded key, which had been sent to George Washington by Lafayette in 1790, was on display in Paris for 10 days before returning to Mount Vernon, where it was rehung in the central passage of the Mansion. The journey marked the first time the key had left Mount Vernon since 1797.

As the year of activities marking the 200th anniversary of Washington's inauguration drew to a close, the Association hosted its first major scholarly conference, "George Washington and the American Presidency," which was co-sponsored by the Founders Society of the American Studies Center. The conference attracted scholars, journalists and political leaders, who analyzed Washington's lasting influence on the nation's highest office by addressing such topics as Washington's relationship with his cabinet and Congress, his military career and his skill as a businessman and plantation owner.

## LOOKING TO THE FUTURE

At its Grand Council meeting in 1987, the Association initiated a Planning and Resources study, to review the status of the current operations and chart a general course for future projects and programs. The two-year project began with an examination of the "essence" of George Washington as the means of defining the central themes of Washington's character that should be the basis of the presentation of Mount Vernon to the public. With this as the basic foundation, the Planning and Resources Committee went on to examine nearly every phase of the Mount Vernon operation, from research and restoration to marketing.

In its first phase, the study reached the reassuring conclusion that though methods and perspective change with the times, the Association remains faithful to its original mission set forth in its charter of 1858.

At the same time, this self-study has raised new questions and challenges for the Association. Visitor surveys reveal changing expectations on the part of the general public and a desire for even-more information about Washington and daily life at Mount Vernon. This is especially true among visitors during the busy spring and summer seasons, when the physical restraints of the Mansion limit the length of the traditional interpretation. The size of the crowds is in itself evidence that George Washington continues to inspire and fascinate people from all over the world. As the new century approaches, the Association's challenge is to find new ways of enhancing the public's understanding of Washington's life and times.

At 138 years old and counting, the Mount Vernon Ladies' Association continues to prove itself as a vibrant and modern organization, able to respond to a pace of change that accelerates with each passing decade, while preserving the traditions of its past.

## Extracts from the Letters and Diaries of George Washington Pertaining to the Development of Mount Vernon

irst in war, first in peace, and first in the hearts of his countrymen"—every American can recite this tribute to George Washington. Many can identify the author, some can relate the circumstances under which the words were spoken. Few can complete the sentence—"he was second to none in the humble and endearing scenes of private life."

Henry Lee, "Light-Horse Harry" of Revolutionary fame, was a member of Congress in 1799 when the melancholy tidings of Washington's death reached Philadelphia, then the seat of the federal government. Lee, neighbor, companion-in-arms, and intimate friend, was eminently qualified to deliver the memorial address from which the above lines are taken. The sentence deserves to be perpetuated in its entirety with the emphasis where the speaker intended, for the final clause is the key to the character of George Washington: "he was second to none...."

George Washington thought of the world as a stage and of himself as a player in his public careers. History has securely recorded the greatness of George Washington, the general and the president, but his very success in these roles has tended to obscure the human traits of the man who played them. The virtue of Mount Vernon, its greatest significance for modern Americans, is that it survives as the embodiment of his taste and evidence of his creative ability in realms of his own choosing.

The master of Mount Vernon was a methodical diarist when at home and a regular correspondent with his managers when away. The six volumes of his published diaries and numerous editions of his papers will richly reward the student in search of George Washington, paterfamilias, farmer, and neighbor, but the record is so extensive and so much other subject matter in intermingled as to discourage the general reader. The following extracts from his diaries, letters, and accounts have been selected to tell the story, in his own words, of the development of Mount Vernon. They begin with the year 1757, when the writer was a young lieutenant colonel in command of Virginia troops defending the western frontiers of the colonies against the depredations and atrocities of the Indians. They end 30 years later when the installation of the Mansion weather vane marked the substantial completion of a development program begun in 1773. The fact the George Washington never consciously devoted himself to this theme imposes a limitation on the continuity of the story; the fact that his writings failed to survive in their entirety imposes another. The annals of Mount Vernon are particularly meager for the pre-Revolutionary period. These years, coinciding with what has been called Virginia's "Golden Age," were happy years, relatively carefree and unclouded by forebodings of responsibilities to come.

As a group these selections reveal George Washington in the role of his own happy choice. It follows that they reflect his character and taste more clearly than do his writings on any other subject. From 1757, when he specified, "Let them be fashionable, neat, and good in their several kinds," to the end of his life, there is evident a discrimination that is rare for the time and place. To one familiar with the beauty, order, and dignity of Mount Vernon this is not surprising. For the discerning reader there is apparent also that greatness of character that contributed so indispensably to the founding of this free nation.

Fort Loudoun, April 15; 1757

...let them be fashionable, neat, and good in their several kinds.

Invoice of sundry goods to be ship'd
by Mr. Washington of London for the
use of G. Washington, Viz.

Fort Loudoun, April 15th, 1757

A Marble Chimney piece of the Dimensions of the Inclos'd (given
by the Workmen) the Cost not to exceed 15 Guineas. N.B. let
it be carefully pack'd.

A Neat Landskip 3 feet by 21 ½ Inches—1 Inch Margin for a Chim'y
250 panes window Glass 11 by 9 Paper for 5 rooms of the following
Dimensions (viz) 18 by 12 16 by 12. 16 by 14; 18 by 15; and 15
by 16, all 8 feet pitch, the Paper differing in their Colours; also
paper of a very good kind and colour for a Dining Room 18 by
16 above Chair boards the pitch of the Room is 11 Feet.

Papier Machee for the Ceiling of two Rooms, one of them 18 Feet
Square, the other 18 by 16 with Cr. Chimneys

Two neat Mahagony Tables 4 ½ feet square when spread and to
join occasionally 1 Doz'n neat and strong Mahagany Chairs at
21/.

Doz'n fashionable Locks for Partition doors and appurtenances.

1 doz'n fash'e Hinges for the said Doors and 2 pr. larger.

*The "Neat Landskip" ordered at this time still survives over the mantel in
the West Parlor. Richard Washington of London was probably a distant cousin.*

*The house that George Washington twice enlarged and in later years re-
ferred to as "The Mansion" was a modest villa at this period. In the absence of the bachelor owner it was repaired and enlarged from one and
one-half to two and one-half stories under supervision of his younger
brother, John Augustine.*

## To John Augustine Washington

Camp at Rays Town, September 25, 1758

The Floor of my Passage is really an Eye sore to me, I would therefore take it up if good and Seasond Plank could be laid in its place.

---

*George Washington and Martha Dandridge Custis were married on January 6, 1759 and took up residence at Mount Vernon with her two young children, Jacky and Patsy, that April. John Alton was for many years a faithful steward and overseer.*

## To John Alton

Thursday Morning, [April 1, 1759]

Jno: I have sent Miles on to day, to let you know that I expect to be up to Morrow, and to get the Key from Colo. Fairfax's which I desire you will take care of. You must have the House very well cleand, and were you to make Fires in the Rooms below it w'd Air them. You must get two of the best Bedsteads put up, one in the Hall Room, and the other in the little dining Room that use to be, and have Beds made on them against we come. You must also get out the Chairs and Tables, and have them very well rubd and Cleand; the Stair case ought also to be polished in order to make it look well.

Enquire abt. in the Neighbourhood, and get some Egg's and Chickens, and prepare in the best manner you can for our coming: you need not however take out any more of the Furniture than the Beds and Tables and Chair's in Order that they may be well rubd and cleand. I am, etc.

Mount Vernon, September 20, 1759

I am now I believe fixd at this Seat with an agreable Consort for Life and hope to find more happiness in retirement than I ever experienc'd amidst a wide and bustling World; I thank you heartily for your Affectionate Wishes; why wont you give me an occasion of Congratulating you in the same manner? None wou'd do it with more cordiality, and true sincerity than, Dear Sir, &c.

Invoice  of  Sundries  to  be  sent  by Robert  Cary  and  Company  for  use  of George  Washington

Mount Vernon, September 20, 1759

8 Busts, according to the Inclosd directin and Measure.

Directions for the Busts.

4. one of Alexr the Great; another of Julius Caesar; anr. of Chs. 12. Sweden; and a 4th of the King of Prussia.

N. B. these are not to exceed 15 Inches in hight, nor 10 in width.

2 other Busts, of Prince Eugene and the Duke of Marlborh, somewhat smaller.

2 Wild Beasts, not to exceed 12 Inches in hight, nor 18 in length.

Sundry Small Ornaments for chimy piece.

*Busts of the subjects listed were not available at the specified sizes. Two plaster lions, which are displayed in traditional position over the east doorway of the central passage, are believed to be the "Wild Beasts" listed in the above order.*

*Robert Cary and Company, of London, were typical of the English factors who bought and sold for planters in Britain's distant colonies.*

To Robert Cary & Company

November 30, 1759

Gentn: By the George and Captns. Richardson and Nicks who saild with the Fleet in September last I sent Invoices of such Goods as were wanting for myself Estate &cta. but knowing that the latter unfortunately founderd at Sea soon after her Departure from Virginia and that the former may probably have sufferd by that Storm or some other accident, by which means my Letters &cta would miscarry I take this oppertunity by way of Bristol of addressing Copies of them, and over and above the things there wrote for to desire the favour of you to send me a neat Grait (for Coal or small Faggots) in the newest taste and of a Size to fit a Chimney abt. 3 feet wide and two Deep, and a fender suited to Ditto, Steel I believe are most usd at present.

*Dr. Craik and Dr. Ross had both been Washington's companions-in-arms during the French and Indian War. Both were to be associated with him in the Revolution. Dr. Craik attended him in his fatal illness. These diary entries and an order a year earlier for "Longley's [Langley's] Book of Gardening" are the earliest evidence of an interest in gardening that was to continue and intensify through the years.*

JANUARY 1760 *Monday, 7th* Wrote from thence [Alexandria] to Doctr. Craik to endeavour, if possible, to engage me a Gardener from the Regiment and returnd in the dusk of the Evening.

*Friday, 25th* Wrote to Doctr. Ross to purchase me a joiner, Bricklayer, and Gardner, if any Ship of Servants was in.

MARCH 1760 22 Transplanted to the Corner of the Borders by Garden House a Cherry Graft—from the Cherry tree at the other Corner of the said Bord by the first Fall.

*The following interesting but incomplete reference indicates that the smaller house of the pre-Revolutionary period had four principal out-buildings or "offices" on a plan similar to that of Stratford, home of the Lees, although on a much smaller scale. These buildings were displaced later, but foundations of two of them survive.*

MARCH 1760 *Thursday,* 27 Agreed to give Mr. William Triplet £18 to build the two houses in the Front of my House (plastering them also), and running walls for Pallisades to them from the Great house and from the Great House to the Wash House and Kitchen also.

APRIL 1760 *Saturday, 5th* Planted out 20 young Pine trees at the head of my Cherry Walk.

JANUARY 1769 9 At home all day, opening the Avenue to the House, and for bringing the Road along.

*"Hell hole" was a poorly drained ravine between the house and the outer, or west gate. It extended to the river shore. In George Washington's time this area was a prime breeding place for mosquitoes, unsuspected trans-mitters of the malaria that afflicted all who lived at Mount Vernon. Mod-ern dredging equipment has made possible the conversion of Hell Hole into a grassy meadow that belies the name it still bears.*

FEBRUARY 1769 25 Finish'd the New road, leadg. across Hell hole, to the House.

To ROBERT CARY & COMPANY

Mount Vernon, November 22, 1771

Captns. of Ships (Johnstoun in particular) I know make a practise of engaging Tradesmen of difference kinds upon Indenture for four or five years and bring them over from whence I conclude a Gardner may be had in the same way but rather than fail I would give moderate wages. I do not desire any of your fine fellows who will content themselves with Planning of Work, I want a Man that will labour hard, knowing at the sametime how to keep a Garden in good Order and Sow Seed in their proper Seasons in ground that he has prepard well for the reception of them.

*The Maryland artist, Charles Willson Peale, painted his first portrait of Washington at Mount Vernon in 1772. At that time he also did miniatures of Mrs. Washington and her two children. Washington's diary and ledger contain these references. It was the custom at that time for artists to move about the country and stay at the homes of wealthy planters while they painted their portraits. All four of these Peale pictures painted at Mount Vernon during this visit are extant today.*

MAY 1772
20 I sat to have my Picture drawn.
21 I set again to take the Drapery.
22 Set for Mr. Peale to finish my Face.

1772
May 30 By Mr. Peale Painter, Drawg. my Picte     £18. 4. 0
Miniature Do. for Mrs. Washington     £13.
Ditto Do. for Miss Custis     13.
Ditto Do. for Mr. Custis     13.
    £57. 4. 0

*The repairs and alterations alluded to below were but the first phases of a sweeping plan that contemplated enlargement of the house and redevelopment of the surrounding area, grounds, gardens, and buildings, on an expanded scale.*

Mount Vernon, October 6, 1773

Gentn: I am almost ashamd to trouble you, in the same year, with such frequent Orders for Goods; but as I am under a necessity of making some repairs to, and alterations in my House, and did not get an Acct. before from the Undertaker of all the Materials wanting it must plead my Excuse for requesting you to send me the undermentioned Articles....

For Geo: Washington
100 Sqrs. of best Crown Glass 9 by 11
A Cask of Whiting
400 Wt. of White Lead ground in Oyl over and above the last Order.
30 lb red Lead. 2 lb Lampblack
100 lb yellow Oaker; 10 lb Umber
20 Gallns. best Brittish Lintseed Oyl for Inside painting
9 pr. dovetail Mortice Hinges mid: size
3 pr. Ditto larger
9 Comm. brass cased Locks 3 Do dble. Spd. best Do
3 M 2d. Brads 3 M 3d. Do 6 M 4d.
Do 6M 6d. Do 8M Clasp Nails instead of Brads for Flooring
40 M 4d. Nails 100 lbs of Lead for Windows and 50 fathom Sash Line.
25 Lbs. best Glew ½ a Ton of unprepd. Plaist'r of Paris

To  Bryan  Fairfax

Mount Vernon, July 4, 1774

Dear Sir: John has just delivered to me your favor of yesterday, which I shall be obliged to answer in a more concise manner, than I could wish, as I am very much engaged in raising one of the additions to my house, which I think (perhaps it is fancy) goes on better whilst I am present, than in my absence from the workmen.

*Bryan Fairfax was the somewhat eccentric younger brother of George William Fairfax of Belvoir. Both brothers and their families were on intimate neighborly terms with the Mount Vernon family.*

*In 1773 Colonel and Mrs. Fairfax left Belvoir for England, never to return, and it is not difficult to imagine the regret felt by all at nearby Mount Vernon, when their ship dropped down the Potomac and out to sea. The two families had been close, and it is not surprising that the Washingtons bought a number of the furnishings of Belvoir, which were sold during the following year. An inventory of their purchases includes the following items.*

|  | £ |
|---|---|
| 2 doz. Mountain Wine | 1. 4. |
| 10 Pewter water Plates | 1. 6. 0 |
| 1 Mahog<sup>y</sup>. Shaving Desk | 4. 0. 0 |
| 1 Sittee bed and furniture | 13. 0. 0 |
| 4 Mahog<sup>y</sup>. Chairs. . .in all | 4. 0. 0 |
| 1 Chamber Carpett | 1. 1. 0 |
| 1 Oval Glass w<sup>t</sup>. Guilt frame in the Green room | 4. 5. 0 |
| 1 Mahog<sup>y</sup>. Chest & drawers in Mrs. F's Chamber | 12.10. 0 |
| 1 Mahog<sup>y</sup>. Side board | 12. 5. 0 |
| 1 Mahog<sup>y</sup>. Cistreen & Stand | 4. 0. 0 |
| 12 Chairs & 3 Window Curtains from y<sup>e</sup> dining room | 11. 0. 0 |
| 1 looking Glass & Guilt frame | 13. 5. 0 |
| 2 Candlesticks & a bust of the Immortal Shakespear | 1. 1. 0 |
| 1 Large Carpett | 11. 0. 0 |
| 1 pr Andirons tonges Fender & Shovell | 3.10. 0 |
| 1 pair of Dogs in the Great Kitchen | 3. 0. 0 |
| 1 Mahog<sup>y</sup> Spider made tea table | 1.11. 0 |
| 1 Carpett | 2.15. 0 |
| 1 large Marble Mortar | 1. 1. 0 |
| a Mahog<sup>y</sup>. Card Table | 4. 0. 0 |

*In early May 1775, Washington left Mount Vernon for Philadelphia, as a Virginia delegate to the Second Continental Congress. During the next month he was put in command of the Army. At that time he could not say when he would return home, but he left the estate in charge of his steward. Lund Washington, wartime manager of Mount Vernon, was a distant cousin of his employer. More than 40 of his letters to General Washington for the years 1775–1783 are preserved in the Mount Vernon archives. They contribute indispensably to the annals of the place during this precarious period.*

## To Lund Washington

Camp at Cambridge, August 20, 1775

I wish you would quicken Lanphire and Sears about the Dining Room Chimney Piece (to be executed as mentioned in one of my last Letters) as I could wish to have that end of the House compleately finished before I return.—I wish you had done the end of the New Kitchen next the Garden as also the Old Kitchen with rusticated Boards; however, as it is not, I would have the Corners done so in the manner of our new Church. (those two especially which Fronts the Quarter). What have you done with the Well?—is that walled up?

## To Lund Washington

[Cambridge, Mass.], November 26, 1775

Let the Hospitality of the House, with respect to the poor, be kept up; Let no one go hungry away. If any of these kind of People should be in want of Corn, supply their necessities, provided it does not encourage them in idleness; and I have no objection to your giving my Money in Charity, to the Amount of forty or fifty Pounds a Year, when you think it well bestowed. What I mean, by having no objection is, that it is my desire that it should be done. You are to consider that neither myself or Wife are now in the way to do these good Offices. In all other respects, I recommend it to you, and have no doubts, of your observing the greatest Oeconomy and frugality; as I suppose you know that I do not get a farthing for my services here more than my Expenses; It becomes necessary therefore, for me to be saving at home.

New York, August 19, 1776

Your Works abt. the Home House will go on Slowly I fear as your hands are reduced, and especially if Knowles fails. remember that the New Chimneys are not to smoke. Plant Trees in the room of all dead ones in proper time this Fall. and as I mean to have groves of Trees at each end of the dwelling House, that at the South end to range in a line from the South East Corner to Colo. Fairfax's, extending as low as another line from the Stable to the dry Well, and towards the Coach House, Hen House, and Smoak House as far as it can go for a Lane to be left for Carriages to pass to, and from the Stable and Wharf. from the No. Et. Corner of the other end of the House to range so as to Shew the Barn &ca. in the Neck; from the point where the old Barn used to stand to the No. Et. Corner of the Smiths Shop, and from thence to the Servants Hall, leaving a passage between the Quarter and Shop, and so East of the Spinning and Weaving House (as they used to be called) up to a Wood pile, and so into the yard between the Servts. Hall and the House newly erected; these Trees to be Planted without any order or regularity (but pretty thick, as they can at any time be thin'd) and to consist that at the North end, of locusts altogether. and that at the South, of all the clever kind of Trees (especially flowering ones) that can be got, such as Crab apple, Poplar, Dogwood, Sasafras, Laurel, Willow (especially yellow and Weeping Willow) twigs of which may be got from Philadelphia) and many others which I do not recollect at present; these to be interspersed here and there with ever greens such as Holly, Pine, and Cedar, also Ivy; to these may be added the Wild flowering Shrubs of the larger kind, such as the fringe Tree and several other kinds that might be mentioned. It will not do to Plant the Locust Trees at the North end of the House till the Framing is up, cover'd in, and the Chimney Built; otherwise it will be labour lost as they will get broke down, defaced and spoil'd, But nothing need prevent planting the Shrubery at the other end of the House. Whenever these are Planted they should be Inclosd, which may be done in any manner till I return; or rather by such kind of fencing as used to be upon the Ditch running towards Hell hole; beginning at the Kitchen and running towards the Stable and rather passing the upper Corner; thence round the Dry Well, below the necessary House, and so on to the Hollow by the Wild Cherry tree by the old Barn; thence to the Smiths Shop and so up to the Servants Hall as before described. If I should ever fulfil my Intention it will be to Inclose it properly; the Fence now described is only to prevent Horses &ca. injuring the young Trees in their growth....

Before I conclude I must beg of you to hasten Lanphire about the addition to the No. End of the House, otherwise you will have it open I fear in the cold and wet Weather, and the Brick work to do at an improper Season, neither of which shall I be at all desirous of.

*The grove "of locusts altogether" that Lund planted at the north end of the Mansion is long since gone, but it has been replanted. Each spring a profusion of locust blossoms justifies George Washington's prominent placement of a common native tree.*

*The following passage relates to the addition at the north end of the house and necessary changes in the chimney and the rooms that adjoined the new room.*

To Lund Washington

Col. Morris's, on the Heights of Harlem,
September 30, 1776

With respect to the chimney, I would not have you for the sake of a little work spoil the look of the fireplaces, tho' that in the parlor must, I should think, stand as it does; not so much on account of the wainscotting, which I think must be altered (on account of the door leading into the new building,) as on account of the chimney piece and the manner of its fronting into the room.

The chimney in the room above ought, if it could be so contrived, to be an angle chimney as others are: but I would not have this attempted at the expence of pulling down the partition. —The

Chimney in the new room should be exactly in the middle of it—the doors and every thing else to be exactly answerable and uniform—in short I would have the whole ececuted in a masterly manner.

You ought surely to have a window in the gable end of the new cellar (either under the Venetian window, or one on each side of it).

## To Lund Washington

Decr. 17th. [1776] Ten Miles above the Falls
[of Delaware]

Matters to my view, but this I say in confidence to you, as a friend, wears so unfavorable an aspect (not that I apprehend half so much danger from Howes Army, as from the disaffection of the three States of New York, Jersey and Pennsylvania) that I would look forward to unfavorable Events, and prepare Accordingly in such a manner however as to give no alarm or suspicion to any one; as one step towards it, have my Papers in such a Situation as to remove at a short notice in case an Enemy's Fleet should come up the River. When they are removd let them go immediately to my Brothers in Berkeley....

If I never did, in any of my Letters, desire you to Plant locusts across from the New Garden to the Spinning House as the Wall is to run from the end of the Sunk Wall (and on that side of it next the Quarter) as also as the other Wall from the old Garden gate to the Smoke House or Hen House (and on the lower side of it) I must request it now in this Letter. let them be tall and strait bodyed and about Eight or ten feet to the first Limbs, plant them thick enough for the limbs to Interlock when the Trees are grown for Instance 15 or 16 feet a part.

*Going Lanphire was a local master builder who had been engaged in 1773 to carry forward the enlargement of the Mansion and related construction. His progress at best was irregular and as the effects of inflation became increasingly severe Lund found it necessary to renegotiate the contract, resorting finally to payment in kind.*

## To Lund Washington

Head Quarters, Middle brook, December 18, 1778

With respect to your bargain with Lanphire I can say nothing. I wish every contract that I make, or that is made for me, should be fulfilled according to the strict and equitable meaning of the Parties, and this in the present case you must be a better judge than I.... but from your state of the case, the true and equitable construction of the bargain seems to me to be, that he ought to have the Corn and Wool, but should be obliged to continue his and Servants labor at their present Wages, till the covered ways and such work as was particularized or had in contemplation at the time is finished....

## To Lund Washington

New Windsor, March 28, 1781

How many Lambs have you had this Spring? How many Colts are you like to have? Is your covered ways done? What are you going about next? Have you any prospect of getting paint and Oyl? are you going to repair the Pavement of the Piazza? Is anything doing, or like to be done with respect to the Wall at the edge of the Hill in front of the House? Have you made good the decayed Trees at the ends of the House, in the Hedges, &ca. Have you made any attempts to reclaim more Land for meadow? &ca. &ca. An acct. of these things would be satisfactory to me, and infinitely amusing in the recital, as I have these kind of improvements very much at heart.

*Throughout the entire period of the war Mount Vernon was exposed to destruction by British vessels and the no less destructive raids of Tory partisans who ranged the waters of Chesapeake Bay and its tributaries almost unopposed. For a time in the spring and summer of 1781, there was the added menace of a British army in eastern Virginia under command of Cornwallis. A small force of Continentals under command of Lafayette was sent to Virginia in the early spring to oppose this army.*

*Early in April Alexandrians were much alarmed by the approach of British men-of-war; preparations were hastily made for defense, but the hostile ships turned back below the town. Some days later, from Alexandria, Lafayette sent General Washington a disturbing account of Lund Washington's behavior on this occasion. Lund, he wrote, had made a voluntary offering of provisions. In consequence, Mount Vernon had been spared while the homes of defiant neighbors had been burned.*

## To Lund Washington

New Windsor, April 30, 1781

I am very sorry to hear of your loss; I am a little sorry to hear of my own; but that which gives me most concern, is, that you should go on board the enemys Vessels, and furnish them with refreshments. It would have been a less painful circumstance to me, to have heard, that in consequence of your noncompliance with their request, they had burnt my House, and laid the Plantation in ruins. You ought to have considered yourself as my representative, and should have reflected on the bad example of communicating with the enemy, and making a voluntary offer of refreshments to them with a view to prevent a conflagration.

It was not in your power, I acknowledge, to prevent them from sending a flag on shore, and you did right to meet it; but you should, in the same instant that the business of it was unfolded, have declared, explicitly, that it was improper for you to yield to the request; after which, if they had proceeded to help themselves, *by force,* you could but have submitted (and being unprovided for defence) this was to be prefered to a feeble opposition which only serves as a pretext to burn and destroy.

I am thoroughly perswaded that you acted from your best judgment; and believe, that your desire to preserve my property, and rescue the buildings from impending danger, were your governing motives. But to go on board their Vessels; carry them refreshments; commune with a parcel of plundering Scoundrels, and request a favor by asking the surrender of my Negroes, was exceedingly ill-judged, and 'tis to be feared, will be unhappy in its consequences, as it will be a precedent for others, and may become a subject of animadversion.

I have no doubt of the enemys intention to prosecute the plundering plan they have begun. And, unless a stop can be put to it by the arrival of a superior naval force, I have as little doubt of its ending in the loss of all my Negroes, and in the destruction of my Houses;....

I do not know what Negroes they may have left you; and as I have observed before, I do not know what number they will have left me by the time they have done; but this I am sure of, that you shall never want assistance, while it is in my power to afford it.

*Enroute to Yorktown in 1781 General Washington had his first glimpse of Mount Vernon since the spring of 1775. His diary account of the occasion reflects the urgency of his mission. He stopped at Mount Vernon for a week in November as he journeyed northward after Cornwallis' surrender, but the recent death of Mrs. Washington's son, John Parke Custis, cast a gloom over what might otherwise have been a pleasant domestic interlude after long years of camp and field.*

SEPTEMBER 1781 9th I reached my own Seat at Mount Vernon (distant 120 Miles from the Hd. of Elk) where I staid till the 12th. and in three days afterwards that is on the 15th. reached Williamsburg.

*The "not very considerable loss" alluded to below comprised the stable at the Mansion house and 10 of the most valuable horses on the estate. The cause of the fire is unknown. The structure was a frame stable, which had been built in 1768.*

To The Comte de Rochambeau

Philadelphia, January 8, 1782

I am extremely sorry to hear of the loss of the Palace at Williamsburg by fire, and must beg your Excellency, to accept my warmest acknowledgements for your goodness in accommodating our sick who were deprived of their Hospital by the accident. My loss at Mount Vernon was not very considerable, but I was in the greatest danger of having my House and all the adjacent Buildings consumed.

To Lund Washington

Philadelphia, January 8, 1782

...the little space between the coming and going of the Post, and the number of letters I have to read and write upon those occasions, will not allow me at this time, to say more about the Stable than that I entirely approve your plan for enlarging it, provided the Coach house can be placed in the middle; without which, the House, with large and dble. doors at one end would have an uncouth appearance, the Coach House should be in the middle and a pediment over it, with a door in the pediment for the purpose of receiving hay &ca., but as the length of the House makes no other difference in the rafters and joice than in the number, they may be set about immediately, in the meantime, if you will let me know the exact distance from the inner range of the Garden Wall (which may become part of the gable end of the Stable) to the outer range of the New Coach House, and the range of the other Houses above it, and will also inform me of the size of the last Coach House and stables, and how much too small the latter were. I can then form some plan, and make a disposition of the Doors and Windows, and transmit it to you; you may also, at the time of furnishing me with these materials to work upon, give me your Ideas of a proper plan; and may consult Evans if he is a man capable of design upon the subject.

## To Lund Washington

Newburgh, December 25, 1782

I observe what you say respecting the Flowering Shrubs and other
Ornamental Trees at the No. end of the House, and as the locusts
by the goodness of their growth may lay claim to an establishment
there, I wish that the afore-mentioned shurbs and ornamental and
curious trees may be planted at both ends that I may determine
hereafter from circumstances and appearances which shall be the
grove and which the wilderness. It is easy to extirpate Trees from
any spot but time only can bring them to maturity.

## To Lund Washington

Newburgh, February 12, 1783

I have now to beg that you will not only send me the Account of
your receipts, and expenditures of Specie; but of every kind of
money subsequent to the Acct. exhibited at Valley Forge, which
ended sometime in April 1778.

I want to know before I come home (as I shall come home with
empty pockets whenever Peace shall take place) how Affairs stand
with me, and what my dependence is.

## To Lund Washington

Newburgh Aug$^r$. 13th 1783

I am truly unfortunate that after all the expence I have been at
about my House, I am to encounter the third Edition, with the
trouble & inconvenience of another cover to it, after my re-

turn—That there can have been little attention, or judgment exercised heretofore in covering it, as a fact that cannot admit a doubt; for he must be a miserable artizan or a very great rascal indeed who, after one experim.ᵗ could not tell what kind of shingles were necessary to prevent a common roof from leaking, or how to place them as they ought to be.... If New Shingles are to be used, write to M.ʳ Newton to bespeak them; and let them be got full two feet in length—but I would submit it to the work man if he has any skill in his profession, & the old shingles can be ripped off without Injury, whether shewing less of them will not supply the defect of their shortness—If it will, the Paint & Oil which has been expended on them will, in a great measure be preserved—but *this* is not to be placed in competition with a *tight* cover—or the *look* of the work....

*The victory at Yorktown was followed by two years of weary waiting for a final peace treaty. In late November 1783, the treaty having been ratified, the British garrison in New York embarked and General Washington rode triumphantly into the city. A few days later he bade farewell to his fellow officers at Fraunces Tavern and began his homeward journey. In Philadelphia he bought presents for Mrs. Washington's grandchildren before journeying on to Annapolis, where Congress was sitting. There on December 23 in the old State House he resigned the commission he had received in June 1775. A spectator wrote that "he rode off from the door, intent upon eating his Christmas dinner at home." Accompanied only by two of his former military aides he pushed on rapidly and reached Mount Vernon on Christmas Eve.*

[Annapolis, December 23, 1783]

Having now finished the work assigned me, I retire from the great theatre of Action; and bidding an Affectionate farewell to this August body under whose orders I have so long acted, I here offer my Commission, and take my leave of all the employments of public life.

## TO SAMUEL VAUGHAN

Mount Vernon, January 14, 1784

I found my new room, towards the completion of which you kindly offered your house-joiner, so far advanced in the wooden part of it, the Doors, Windows and floors being done, as to render it unnecessary to remove your workman with his Tools (the distance being great) to finish the other parts; especially as I incline to do it in stucco, (which, if I understood you right, is the present taste in England), and more especially as you may find occasion for him in the execution of your own purposes as the Spring advances. And now my good sir, as I have touched upon the business of stuccoing, permit me to ask you if the rooms with which it is encrusted are painted, generally; or are they left of the natural colour which is given by the cement made according to Mr. Higgins's mode of preparing it? And also, whether the rooms thus finished are stuccoed below the surbase (chair high) or from thence upwards only?

*This is the room about which General Washington had written to Lund from Harlem Heights in 1776. His efforts to have its decoration "executed in a masterly manner" were to continue several years longer.*

*Samuel Vaughan was an Englishman, a friend and admirer of General Washington. At the time the above inquiry was penned he was residing in Philadelphia.*

## To William Hamilton

Mount Vernon, January 15, 1784

Sir: If I recollect right, I heard you say, when I had the pleasure of seeing you last, that you were [thinking] about a floor composed of a cement which was to answer the purpose of Flagstone or Tile, and that you proposed to variegate the colour in the manner of the former.

As I have a long open Gallery in front of my house to which I want to give a stone; or some other kind of floor which will stand the weather, I would thank you for information respecting the success of your experiment with such directions and observations (if you think the method will answer) as would enable me to execute my purpose. If any of the component parts are rare and expensive, please to note it, and where they are to be obtained, and whether all seasons will do for the admixture of the composition. I will make no apology for the liberty I take by this request, as I persuade myself you will not think it much trouble to comply with it. I am etc.

*William Hamilton lived at "Bush Hill," near Philadelphia.*

## To Bushrod Washington

Mount Vernon, January 15, 1784

When I came to examine the Chimney pieces in this House, I found them so interwoven with the other parts of the Work and so good of their kind, as to induce me to lay aside all thoughts of taking any of them down; for the only room which remains unfinished I am not yet fixed in my own mind but believe I shall place a Marble one there. at any rate I shall suspend the purchase of any of those mentioned in your letter, and would not wish Mr. Roberts to hold either of them in expectation of it.

*Bushrod Washington was the older son of General Washington's brother, John Augustine. At the time this letter was written he was studying law in Philadelphia.*

## To Clement Biddle

Mount Vernon, January 17, 1784

I have seen rooms with gilded borders; made I believe, of papier Machi fastned on with Brads or Cement round the Doors and window Casings, Surbase &ca.; and which gives a plain blew, or green paper a rich and handsome look. Is there any to be had in Philadelphia?, and at what price? Is there any plain blew and green Paper to be had also? the price (by the yd. and width)

*Clement Biddle was a Philadelphia merchant.*

*The relationship between the Marquis de Lafayette and George Washington was unique. It is best described by Lafayette himself in a letter of presentation accompanying the key to the Bastille; he wrote, "It is a tribute which I owe as a son to my adopted father—as an aide-de-camp to my general—as a missionary of liberty to its patriarch."*

## To the Marquis de Lafayette

Mount Vernon, February 1, 1784

At length my Dear Marquis I am become a private citizen on the banks of the Potomac, and under the shadow of my own Vine and my own Fig-tree, free from the bustle of a camp and the busy scenes of public life, I am solacing myself with those tranquil enjoyments, of which the Soldier who is ever in pursuit of fame, the Statesman whose watchful days and sleepless nights are spent in devising schemes to promote the welfare of his own, perhaps the ruin of other countries, as if this globe was insufficient for us all, and the Courtier who is always watching the countenance of his Prince, in hopes of catching a gracious smile, can have very little conception. I am not only retired from all public employments, but I am retiring within myself; and shall be able to view the solitary walk, and tread the paths of private life with heartfelt satisfaction. Envious of none, I am determined to be pleased with all; and this my dear friend, being the order for my march, I will move gently down the stream of life, until I sleep with my Fathers.

*Tench Tilghman was a former military aide, for whom George Washington felt a warm attachment. His promising postwar career as a Baltimore merchant was cut short by death in 1786.*

### To Tench Tilghman

Mount Vernon, March 24, 1784

I am informed that a Ship with Palatines is gone up to Baltimore, among whom are a number of Trademen. I am a good deal in want of a House Joiner and Bricklayer, (who really understand their profession) and you would do me a favor by purchasing one of each, for me. I would not confine you to Palatines. If they are good workmen, they may be of Asia, Africa, or Europe. They may be Mahometans, Jews or Christian of an Sect, or they may be Athiests.

### To Clement Biddle

Mount Vernon, June 30, 1784

I shall be obliged to you for sending me 70 yds. of gilded Border for papered Rooms (of the kind you shewed me when I was in Philadelphia). That which is most light and Airy I should prefer. I do not know whether it is usual to fasten it on with Brads or Glew; if the former I must beg that as many be sent as will answer the purpose.

## To John Rumney

Mount Vernon, July 3, 1784

General Washington presents his compliments to Mr. Rumney, would esteem it as a particular favor if Mr. Rumney would make the following enquiries as soon as convenient after his arrival in England, and communicate the result of them by the Packet, or any other safe and speedy conveyance to this Country.

1st. The terms upon which the best kind of Whitehaven Flagstone, black and white in equal quantities, could be delivered at the Generals landing or at the Port of Alexanda. by the superficial foot, with the freight and every other incidental charge included. The Stone to be 2½ inches thick, or there abouts, and exactly a foot square each kind (i.e. black and white), to have a well polished face and good joints, so as that a neat floor may be made for the Colonade in the front of his house. Stone thus prepared must be carefully packed, otherwise the face and edges would be damaged; the expence of which should also be taken into the accot.

2d. Upon what terms the common Irish marble, (black and white if to be had, and of the same dimensions) could be had, delivered as above.

3d. As the General has been informed of a very cheap kind of marble, good in quality wch. is to be had at, or in the neighbourhood of Ostend in France, he would thank Mr. Rumney, if it should fall in his way, to institute the same enquiry respecting this also, and give information thereon.

On the report of Mr. Rumney, the General will take his ultimate determination, for which reason he prays him to be precise. The Piazza or colonade, for which this Stone is wanted as for the purpose of a floor, is ninety two feet eight inches, by twelve feet 8 inches, within the border or margin, which surround it. Over and above this quantity if the Flag is cheap, or a cheaper kind of hard stone could be had, he would get as much as would lay the floors of the circular Colonades at the end wings of the House, each of which in length at the outer curve is 38 feet, by 7 feet 2 inches in breadth within the margin.

*John Rumney was a merchant and shipowner of Whitehaven, England.*

*On the basis of information submitted by Tilghman, General Washington increased the breadth of his unfinished greenhouse. At the General's request Tilghman also sent a plan of the underground flues that heated Mrs. Charles Carroll's greenhouse at Mt. Clare, near Baltimore. This plan, which survives in the Washington papers at the Library of Congress, was followed in the reconstruction of the Mount Vernon greenhouse in 1950.*

### To Tench Tilghman

Mount Vernon, August 11, 1784

I shall essay the finishing of my green house this fall, but find that neither myself, nor any person about me is so well skilled in the internal construction as to proceed without a probability at least of running into errors.

Shall I for this reason, ask the favor of you to give me a short description of the Green-house at Mrs. Carrolls? I am persuaded, now that I planned mine upon too contracted a scale. My house is (of Brick) 40 feet by 24, in the outer dimensions, and half the width disposed of for two rooms, back of the part designed for the green house; leaving the latter in the clear not more than about 37 by 10. As there is no cover on the walls yet, I can raise them to any height.

### To George Augustine Washington

Mount Vernon, January 6, 1785

If it is not too late in the Season to obtain them, I wish you would procure for me in So. Carolina a few of the Acorns of the live Oak, and the Seeds of the Evergreen Magnolia; this latter is called in Millers Gardeners dictionary greater Magnolia, it rises according to his Acct. to the height of Eighty feet or more, flowers early, and is a beautiful tree...

*George Augustine Washington was a favorite nephew of General Washington and for a time was manager of Mount Vernon.*

*The seeds of this Magnolia were secured and the seedlings thrived. A Magnolia planted by General Washington near the courtyard survived until 1918. Several fine specimens descended from this tree are now growing in the plantings about the hilltop.*

*During the winter, spring, and early summer of 1785 George Washington devoted much of his time to development of the planting plan first indicated in his letter to Lund from New York, August 1776. Numerous entries in his diary for this period report the activity in detail. His successes and failures are faithfully noted. These notes have been a useful guide in restoring and maintaining the planting plan developed with so much perseverance by George Washington.*

JANUARY 1785 *Wednesday, 12th* Road to my Mill Swamp, where my Dogue run hands were at Work, and to other places in search of the sort of Trees I shall want for my Walks, groves, and Wildernesses.

JANUARY 1785 *Wednesday, 19th* Employed until dinner in laying out my Serpentine road and Shrubberies adjoining.

To William Grayson

Mount Vernon, January 22, 1785

Did you not my good Sir tell me when I had the pleasure of spending an evening with you at Dumfries, that you either had or could procure me some Scions of the Aspin tree? Are there any young shoots which could be had of the Yew tree, or Hemlock (for I do not now recollect which of these it is) that grows on the Margin of Quantico Creek? Plantations of this kind are now become my amusement and I should be glad to know where I could obtain a supply of such sorts of trees as would diversify the scene.

To  Samuel  Vaughan

Mount Vernon, February 5, 1785

I have the honor to inform you that the Chimney piece is arrived, and by the number of Cases (ten) too elegant and costly by far I fear for my room, and republican stile of living, tho' it encreased the sense of my obligation to you for it. The Ship arrived at her Port just as this second frost set in, so that it has not been in my power to send up for these cases by water; and I would not hazard the transportation of them by land, nine miles.

*This marble mantel was duly installed in the new room and there remains, the most imposing feature of the house. Vaughan later sent three vases to grace the mantel; two of them have been returned by a descendant of Mrs. Washington.*

February 1785 *Tuesday, 22d* Removed two pretty large and full grown Lilacs to the No. Garden gate, one on each side, taking up as much dirt with the roots as cd. be well obtained. Also a mock orange to the walk leading to the No. Necessary.

I also removed from the Woods and the old fields, several young Trees of the Sassafras, Dogwood, and Red bud, to the shrubbery on the No. side the grass plat.

February 1785 *Friday, 25th* Laid of part of the Serpentine Road on the South side the grass plat, to day. Prevented going on with it, first by the coming in of Mr. Michael Stone about 10 Oclock (who went away before noon); then by the arrival of Colo. Hooe, Mr. Chas. Alexander, and Mr. Chas. Lee before dinner, and Mr. Crawford, his Bride, and Sister after it.

FEBRUARY 1785 *Saturday, 26th* Finished laying out my Serpentine roads. Dug most of the holes where the trees by the side of them are to stand, and planted some of the Maple, which were dug yesterday, and some of the Aspan, which had been brought here on Wednesday last.

TO  GEORGE  WILLIAM  FAIRFAX

Mount Vernon, February 27, 1785

Do you think it would be in your power, with ease and convenience, to procure for me, a male and female Deer or two, the cost of transportation I would gladly be at.

*There are many references in General Washington's letters and diaries to the development of a paddock for deer on the slope between the Mansion and the river. An area of about 18 acres was enclosed by a wooden fence and stocked with deer, but the enclosure proved difficult to maintain. The deer escaped and damaged the plantings which were being so painstakingly established. The venture was abandoned after a few years and the deer paddock became an open park.*

*Henry Knox was a former companion-in-arms, general in command of artillery during the Revolution. He was later to be Secretary of War in Washington's cabinet.*

To Henry Knox

Mount Vernon, February 28, 1785

My Gardens have gravel walks (as you possibly may recollect) in the usual Style, but if a better composition has been discovered for these, I should gladly adopt it. the matter however which I wish principally to be informed in, is, whether your walks are designed for Carriages, and if so, how they are prepared, to resist the impression of the Wheels. I am making a serpentine road to my door, and have doubts (which it may be in your power to remove) whether any thing short of solid pavement will answer.

March 1785 *Thursday, 10th* Sent my Waggon with the Posts for the Oval in my Court Yard, to be turned by a Mr. Ellis at the T[u]rng. Mill on Pohick, and to proceed from thence to Occoquan for the Scion of the Hemlock in my Shrubberies.

March 1785 *Friday, 11th* Planted the Hemlock Scions which were brought home yesterday, 28 in number in the shrubbery, 2 poplar trees wch. had been omitted (by an oversight) in my serpentine Walks before; and 13 Weeping and 13 Yellow Willow trees alternately along the Post and Rail fence from the Kitchen to the South ha-haw and from the Servants' Hall to the Smith's Shop.

March 1785 *Tuesday, 15th* Laid out a walk for the wilderness, intended on the No. of the Serpentine road on the right.

Began to open Vistas throu the Pine grove on the Banks of H. Hole.

March 1785 *Saturday, 19th* Received a Swan, 4 wild Geese, and two Barrels of Holly Berries (in Sand) from my brother John, and a Barrel of the early corn from New York.

March 1785 *Thursday, 31st* Planted the Scarlet or French honey suckle (as my Gardner calls it, and which he says blows all the summer) at each Column of my covered ways, as also against the circular walls between the Store house, etca. and the two New Necessaries.

APRIL 1785 Wednesday, 6th Sowed the semicircle North of the front gate with Holly berries sent me by my Brother John—three drills of them: the middle one of Berries which had been got about Christmas and put in Sand, the other two of Berries which had been got earlier in the year, gently dried, and packed in Shavings.

*These holly berries from Bushfield, home of John Augustine Washington on Nomini Creek in Westmoreland County, were intended for hedge plantings in areas adjoining the bowling green. The hedges did not succeed, but two large hollies growing in one of the same areas today are believed to have survived from a planting of this period.*

*Robert Edge Pine, the British artist, arrived at Mount Vernon late in April 1785. During his visit he painted the portrait of Fanny Bassett, niece of Mrs. Washington, and those of the four Custis grandchildren. The following diary and letter references refer to the pictures. Several of these Pine portraits hang at Mount Vernon today.*

APRIL 1785 *Thursday, 28th* To Dinner Mr. Pine, a pretty eminent Portrait and Historical Painter, arrived in order to take my picture from the life.... This Gentleman stands in good estimation as a Painter in England.

DECEMBER 1785 *Saturday, 31st...* had brought from Alexandria the Picture drawn by Mr. Pine of Fanny Bassett now Washington and the young Custis.

## To Robert Edge Pine

Mount Vernon, February 26, 1786

The pictures arrived shortly after in good order, and meet the approbation of Mrs. Washington and myself, the first of whom thanks you for the portrait of Fanny Washington, with which you have been so polite to present her....

It is some time since I requested a Gentleman of Annapolis...to pay you Twenty guineas and sixteen Dollars; the first for balance due on the pictures, the latter for their frames....

### To John Rumney

Mount Vernon, June 22, 1785

I delayed making choice of either of the samples of Flagstone, until I had seen the Irish marble, and was made acquainted with the cost of it; but as it is not yet arrived, and I like the whitest and cheapest of the three samples wch. you sent me by Capt. Atkinson, I request the favor of you to forward by the first opportunity (with some to spare in case of breakage or other accidents) as much of this kind as will floor the Gallery in front of my house, which within the margin, or border that goes round it, and is already laid with a hard stone of the County, is 92 feet 7 ½ inches, by 12 feet 9 ¼ inches.

### To John Rawlins

Mount Vernon, August 29, 1785

I have a room 32 by 24 feet, and 16 feet pitch, which I want to finish in stucco; it is my intention to do it in a plain neat style; which, independantly of its being the present taste, (as I am inform'd) is my choice. The Chimney is in the centre of the longest side, for which I have a very elegant marble piece; directly opposite thereto is a Venetian window, of equal breadth and pitch of the room; on each side of the chimney is a door, leading into other rooms, and on each of the short sides is a door and window.

156

I mention these things that you may be apprized of the sort of work; the time it may take you to execute it, and that you may inform me upon what terms; and also, if you are inclined to undertake it, that you may have leisure to think of a design. The season being so far advanced, I had given up the idea of doing anything to the room this year; but if I could enter upon the work with well founded assurances of accomplishing it soon, I am ready and willing to go on with it immediately; having by me stucco, and seasoned plank for the floor and other parts (if necessary) and good Joiners of my own to execute what may be wanting in their way.

*John Rawlins (or Rawlings) of Baltimore, was a contractor, or "undertaker," in decorative plaster work.*

SEPTEMBER 1785 *Thursday, 29th* Mr. Sanders, an Undertaker in Alexandria, came down between breakfast and Dinner to advise a proper mode of shingling, putting Copper in the Gutters between the Pediments and Dormants, and the Roof, and to conduct the Water along the Eves to Spouts, and promised to be down again on Tuesday next to see the Work properly begun.

OCTOBER 1785 *Sunday, 2d* After we were in Bed (about eleven Oclock in the Evening) Mr. Houdon, sent from Paris by Doctr. Franklin and Mr. Jefferson to take my Bust, in behalf of the State of Virginia, with three young men assistants, introduced by a Mr. Perin a French Gentleman of Alexandria, arrived here by Water from the latter place.

*This incident might seem to have no relation to the theme of these extracts, but the arrival of Jean Antoine Houdon, the outstanding sculptor of his day, at this distant estate was an important event in the annals of Mount Vernon and the history of Washington portraiture—too interesting to be ignored.*

*Houdon completed his mission and left Mount Vernon on the 19th. His first medium was clay; the bust which he modeled in this medium was copied in plaster. The plaster was taken back to France for reproduction;*

*the clay bust was relinquished to his subject and has survived to be recognized by critics as the best likeness of General Washington. It was presented to the Mount Vernon Ladies' Association by the last private owner of Mount Vernon, John Augustine Washington, Jr., and is the central feature of the present museum.*

OCTOBER 1785 *Thursday, 6th* Mr. Sanders not coming according to Expectation I began with my own people to shingle that part of the Roof of the House wch. was stripped yesterday; and to copper the Gutters, &ca.

*The shingle roof that General Washington completed at this time served until the 1860s, when it was replaced by the Association. This covering served until 1912, when the house was again re-roofed. The hand-rived cypress shingles placed at that time were in service until the 1970s, when cypress was unavailable for another re-roofing, and western cedar was substituted.*

OCTOBER 1785 *Friday, 28th* Finished levelling and Sowing the lawn in front of the Ho. intended for a Bolling Green—as far as the Garden Houses.

November 1785 *Saturday, 12th* Covered my exotic plants in that section of my Botanical Garden between the Salt House and the House next the Circle; and began to cover the Guinea grass, which two days before I had cut of near the Crown, but did not finish it.

NOVEMBER 1785 *Wednesday, 16th* Finished the Arch over my Ice House to day.

DECEMBER 1785 *Saturday, 3rd* Finished covering my Ice House with dirt and sodding of it.

JANUARY 1786 *Friday, 13th* Laid out the ground behind the Stable, formerly a Vineyard, for a fruit Garden.

FEBRUARY 1786 *Saturday, 4th* Having assembled the Men from my Plantations, I removed the garden Houses which were in the middle of the front walls to the extreme points of them; which were done with more ease and less damage than I expected, considering the height one of them was to be raised from the ground.

*These small octagonal structures still stand at the west end of the formal gardens where General Washington placed them in 1786.*

FEBRUARY 1786 *Saturday, 11th* Brought a Goose and Gander of the Chinese breed of Geese, from the Reverend Mr. Griffiths; and also two of the large white (or Portugal) Peach trees; and 2 Scions from a tree growing in his garden, to which he could give no name—the last for my Shrubberies.

FEBRUARY 1786 *Saturday, 18th* Began the yards back of the Green house designed for the Jack Ass and Magnolia.

*The jackass, Royal Gift, was a present from the King of Spain. Magnolia was an Arab stallion. General Washington is reported to have been the first American to breed mules.*

MARCH 1786 *Monday, 13th* The ground being in order for it, I set the people to raising and forming the mounds of Earth by the gate in order to plant Weeping Willow thereon.

*These mounds exist today and weeping willows still grow on them. This variety of willow was a recent importation in 1786. General Washington was following the fashions in landscape gardening of his day.*

MARCH 1786 *Saturday, 25th* In removing the planks about the Venetian Window, at the North end of the house, the Sill, and ends of the Posts, and studs, were found decayed; and were accordingly, the first renewed, and the other repaired.

*This repair was uncovered in 1932. The ends of the posts had been cut obliquely and spliced, being dependent for bearing capacity on the spikes that joined them to the replaced section. A more effective splice was substituted.*

MARCH 1786 *Thursday, 30th* Planted in the holly clumps, in my shrubberies a number of small holly trees which some months ago Colo. Lee of Stratford sent me in a box with earth; also in the same shrubberies some of the slips of the Tree box. I also planted several holly trees which had been sent to me the day before by a neighbour, Mr. Thos. Allison.

*One of the tree box plants sent by Colonel Lee, "Light Horse Harry," is still growing on the bowling green, opposite the kitchen garden gate. Two others in the shrubbery nearby may have the same origin although they are smaller. The specimen on the bowling green is perhaps the handsomest "living link" between Mount Vernon and George Washington.*

APRIL 1786 *Wednesday 19th* Before dinner, Mr. Rollins and a Mr. Tharpe came here. The first being the undertaker of my new room intended to commence the work, and then to leave it under the conduct of the latter, which I objected to for reasons which I assigned him; he therefore determined to return and come back prepared to attend to it himself.

MAY 1786 *Wednesday, 3d* Perceived the Seeds of the Honey locust to be coming up, irregularly—whether owing to their being shallowest planted, hardness of the ground, or not I cannot say.

*These honey locust seedlings were also intended for use as hedges or "live fences" in the area about the Mansion house.*

MAY 1786 *Tuesday, 23d* And this day began to lay the Flags in my Piaza—Cornelius and Tom Davis assisting.

*These stones were imported from an English quarry. Many of the original stones laid at this time still form a part of the piazza pavement. Others,*

*worn out by the millions of feet which have trod the piazza, have been re-*
*placed by duplicate stones drawn from a supply cut in the same English*
*quarry just before World War I.*

*James Bloxham was engaged on recommendation of Washington's former*
*neighbor, George William Fairfax, who was living in England. The con-*
*tract was renewed and Bloxham's family followed him across the ocean, but*
*the Englishman was a disappointment. By mutual agreement he resigned*
*his responsibility and returned to England in 1790.*

    *George Washington was strongly influenced by English methods in his*
*practice of agriculture and was hopeful that Bloxham would introduce re-*
*forms which would improve his farms. But Bloxham, finding himself un-*
*able to cope with conditions so alien to his experience, fell into the same lax*
*habits he had been engaged to remedy.*

### AGREEMENT WITH JAMES BLOXHAM

[Mount Vernon] May 31, 1786

Articles of Agreement entered into this 31st. day of May in the year
1786 between George Washington Esqr. of the County of Fairfax
and Commonwealth of Virginia of the one part, and James Bloxham
lately from the Shire of Gloucester in the Kingdom of England
Farmer of the other part. Witnesseth, That the said James Bloxham
for and in consideration of the wages, allowances, and priviledges
hereinafter mentioned, doth agree with, and oblige himself to serve,
the said George Washington for the space of one year; to commence the first day of the present Month, in the capacity of a
Farmer and Manager of such parts of Husbandry, as shall be committed to his charge; and will, to the utmost of his skill and abilities,
order and direct the same (with the approbation of the said George
Washington) to the best advantage. That he will, at all times, and
upon all occasions, suggest such plans for the improvement of the
said Washington Farms, and the stocks of Horses, Cattle, Sheep,

Hogs &ca. which are on them, as to him shall appear most conducive to his interest. Will keep regular Accts. of the said Stock, and will strictly observe and follow all such orders and directions as he shall, from time to time, receive from his said employer; for this, and for other purposes. That when thereunto required, he will buy, at the expence of the said Washington, Cattle or Sheep for feeding, or for Store; and will dispose of the same, or any others, to the best advantage; attending particularly to the care and management of the Stock of every kind, both in Winter and Summer, as well those for the use and benefit of the Farms, and for family consumption, as those which may be fatted for Market. That he will use his utmost endeavours to encrease, and properly distribute, the Manure in the farms; and also will improve to the best of his judgment, the impliments of husbandry necessary thereto, and will instruct, as occasion may require, and opportunity offer, the labourers therein how to Plow, Sow, Mow, reap, Thatch, Ditch, Hedge &ca. in the best manner. And generally, That he will consider the said Washingtons interest as his own, and use his true endeavour to promote it accordingly. In consideration whereof, the said George Washington doth agree to pay the said James Bloxham Fifty Guineas for his years Services, to be compleated on the first day of May 1787; and will allow him the said Bloxham, ten guineas besides, towards defraying the expences of bringing his wife and family to this Country. That when they shall have arrived, he will provide him, and them, a decent and comfortable House to reside in, by themselves; will lend them two Cows for Milk, a Sow to raise Pigs for their own eating (but not to sell), and give them as much Bran as is sufficient to brew Beer for his family, use. And moreover, will allow them for the part of the year which will remain after the arrival of his family and leaving his present board, at the rate of Six hundred pounds of Porke or Beef, and Eight hundred pounds of middling flour, per Annum, and likewise a piece of ground sufficient for a Garden, and firewood. The said George Washington also agrees to provide the said James Bloxham with a horse to ride on for the purpose of superintending the business herein required. or, if the said Bloxham shall find his own horse, to allow pasturage, and reasonable feed for him. Lastly, it is agreed between the said George Washington and James Bloxham, that if the said James should not return to England at the expiration of the year for which he now engages, and his conduct shall be such as to merit the approbation of the said George Washington, that then, and in those cases, his wages for the next year shall be Sixty Guineas; and the other allowances and privileges the same as those of the present year. In testimony of all, and each of these Articles, and for the full and perfect compliance therewith, the parties to these presents hath interchangeably set their hands and Seals, and to the other, doth bind himself in the Sum of One hundred pounds Currt. Money of Virginia, the day and year first written.

JUNE 1786 *Friday, 16th* Began about 10 Oclock to put up the Book press in my study.

*This built-in bookcase was intended to house Washington's growing library. Ultimately his collection of books numbered over a thousand volumes. The titles indicate a preference for practical subjects, but religion, philosophy, history and the ancient classics were well represented. A library of this size and scope was a great rarity in 18th-century Virginia.*

To JOSEPH DASHIELL

Mount Vernon, June 21, 1786

I thank you for requesting a skipper from the Eastern shore to call upon, and make me an offer of the posts and rails he had for sale. They were not however of a kind to answer my purposes (being for paling), nor should I incline to buy any unless they are better *and are to be had cheaper* than those wch. might be taken from my own land. To judge of the propriety of this, you wou'd oblige me Sir, by informing me on what terms Cypress posts 7 feet long, 5 inches by 6 at top and 7 inches by 6 at bottom; (a stock a foot square making 4), and Cypress plank 12 feet long, 6 wide and 1 ¼ inches thick, could be had delivered at my landing, supposing 500 of the first, and a proportional quantity of the latter for rails. I mention cypress on a supposition that it is a lasting wood for posts; but would be glad to know also, *what the difference in price would be, between cypress and Pine, in the rails only.* This letter supplies the specifications for the plank fences used at Mount Vernon today. An early view supplies the additional information that there were four rails to a panel.

*The addressee is identified as Joseph Dashiell of Salisbury, Maryland. Washington was always troubled by the spelling of proper names, though his spelling improved through the years. In another instance he referred to this correspondent as Mr. Joseph De Shields.*

To George William Fairfax

Mount Vernon, June 26, 1786

Tho' envy is no part of my composition, yet the picture you have drawn of your present habitation and mode of living is enough to create strong desires in me to be a participator of the tranquility and rural amusements you have described. I am getting into the latter as fast as I can, being determined to make the remainder of my life easy, let the world or the affairs of it go as they may. I am not a little obliged to you for the assurance of contributing to this, by procuring me a Buck and Doe of the best English deer; but if you have not already been at this trouble, I would my good Sir, now wish to relieve you from it, as Mr. Ogle of Maryland has been so obliging as to present me six fawns from his park of English deer at Belle air. Of the Forest deer of this Country, I have also procured six, two bucks and four does; with these, and tolerable care, I shall soon get into a full stock from my small paddock. I do not mean to comprehend in this relinquishment, the offer of my good friend Mrs. Fairfax. I will receive with great pleasure and gratitude the seeds of any trees or shrubs wch. are not natives of this country, but reconcilable to the climate of it, that she may be so obliging as to send me; and while my attentions are bestowed on the nurture of them, it would, if anything was necessary to do it, remind me of the happy moments I have spent in conversations on this and other subjects with that Lady at Belvoir. . . . So many come here without *proper* introductions, that it is a real satisfaction when I am able to discriminate; this will be the case whenever Mr. Ansty or any other shall present a letter to me from you. My manner of living is plain. I do not mean to be put out of it, a glass of wine and a bit of mutton are always ready, and such as will be content to partake of them are welcome, those who expect more will be disappointed, but no change will be affected by it.

To Clement Biddle

Mount Vernon, September 23, 1786

It is sometime since my window curtains were sent to you to get dyed; I should be glad to have them back as soon as an opportunity offers of forwarding them to me. Let me beg you to send by Mr. Porter, (who will deliver you this letter) if he can bring it, or with the curtains if he cannot, 16 yards of Stuff of the same kind and colour of the curtains, to cover two dozen chairs, the front of which will require cloth near 2 ½ feet wide, and the hinder part near two feet; this I fear is wider than that kind of Stuff generally is, but it is to be hoped that the gores which come off the latter, will be sufficient for the former.

OCTOBER 1786 *Tuesday, 17th* At home all day. Began to set a brick kiln.

*All of the bricks used at Mount Vernon were molded and burned on the place.*

*George Digges was a neighbor on the Maryland shore of the Potomac. His home, Warburton Manor, stood at the mouth of Piscataway Creek in view of Mount Vernon. There was frequent communication between the two places as members of the households, their guests, and recommended travelers were ferried back and forth.*

*Early in the 19th century Warburton Manor became Fort Washington and the dismantled fort, which commands a magnificent view of the river, is now administered by the National Park Service.*

### To George Digges

Mount Vernon, December 28, 1786

Will you allow me to give you the trouble of enquiring among your friends of the Eastern shore, now at Annapolis, if I could be furnished with one thousand feet of the best pine plank, precisely 24 feet long when dressed, to be without knots or sap. It is for the floor of my new room. Many years ago I provided for this, and thought myself secure of that which was perfectly seasoned. It had been dressed and laid by; but when I was about to make use of it, behold! two thirds of it was stolen, and the other ⅓ will match no plank I can now get.

April 1787, *Tuesday, 3d* Brought the Ditchers to the home house to finish the New Road, and to compleat the sunk fence in front of the Lawn.

*Sunk fences, or "ha has," were constructed at three points about the house to complete the division between the formal planted area and the adjoining meadows, farm enclosures, and park. These barriers had the virtue of stopping cattle without interrupting the view.*

Mount Vernon, April 13, 1787

I have received the freizes for the doors and windows which I think are very pretty, together with your letter sent by Capt. Man, but I did not think proper to comply with the contents of it at this time. Altho' it is not my desire to enter into any dispute respecting the payment of the money, yet before I do it I wish you to view the work, that you may, yourself judge of the execution. My sole motive for employing Mr. Tharp to execute the common plaster work, and giving a higher price than what I could have had it done for by others, was the expectation, that, agreeable to promise, it would have been done in a masterly manner; but this is not the case, and you would think so yourself, was you to see it, the Stucco work in the Parlour is much cracked and Stained, the plain work in the New Room and in every other part of the House, is in fact but little better than the plaster which was pulled down. Mr. Tharp said something should be done to hide the Stains and blemishes, but that it was not proper to do it when he was here, this I expect will be performed. There is likewise wanting to compleat the New Room 6 doz large hollows, 3 doz dble F. O. G. and 6 feet of fluting, some person was to have been sent by you to decorate the pilasters, which has not yet been done. When the work is compleated and your engagement properly fulfil you will find on my part no inclination to withhold the pay.

Agreement with Philip Bater

April 23, 1787

Articles of Agreement made this twelveth day of April Anno Domini one thousand seven hundred and eighty-seven, by and between George Washington Esqr. of the Parish of Truro, in the County of Fairfax, State of Virginia, on the one part and Philip

Bater, Gardner, on the other Witness, that the said Philip Bater, for and in consideration of the covenants herein, hereafter, mentioned, doth promise and agree to serve the sd. George Washington, for the term of one year, as a Gardner, and that he will, during said time, conduct himself soberly, diligently and honestly, that he will faithfully and industriously perform all, and every part of his duty as a Gardner, to the best of his knowledge and abilities, and that he will not, at any time, suffer himself to be disguised with liquor, except on the times hereafter mentioned.

In Consideration of these things being well and truly performed on the part of the sd. Philip Bater, the said George Washington doth agree to allow him (the sd. Philip) the same kind and quantity of provisions as he has heretofore had; and likewise, annually a decent suit of clothes befitting a man in his station; to consist of a Coat, Vest and breeches; a working Jacket and breeches, of homespun, besides; two white Shirts; three Check Do; two pair of yarn Stockings; two pair of Thread Do; two linnen Pocket handkerchiefs; two pair of linnen overalls; as many pair of Shoes as are actually necessary for him; four Dollars at Christmas, with which he may be drunk 4 days and 4 nights; two Dollars at Easter to effect the same purpose; two Dollars also at Whitsontide, to be drunk two days; A Dram in the morning, and a drink of Grog at Dinner or at Noon.

For the true and faithful performance of all and each of these things the parties have hereunto set their hands this twenty third day of April Anno Domini 1787.

To George Augustine Washington

Philadelpa., June 10, 1787

Desire Matthew to give me the exact dimension of the windows (one will do) of the dining room; within the casement (in the room) that I may get a Venetion blind, such as draws up and closes, and expands made here, that others may be made by it, at home. the height from the bottom to top, and width is all that is necessary within the casement.

To George Augustine Washington

Philadelphia, July 29, 1787

I desire that the honey suckles against the Houses and brick walls, may be nailed up; and made to spread regularly over them. Should those near the Pillars of the Colonades or covered ways, be dead, their plants should be supplied with others; as I want them to run up, and Spread over the parts which are painted green.

To George Augustine Washington

Philadelphia 12th Aug$^t$. 1787

By the Dolphin, Captn. Steward, I have sent some Goods and other articles round; which I hope will arrive safe.—Among them, is the top for the Cupulo of the House, which has been left so long unfinished.—I do not suppose there would have been any difficulty in fixing it without direction; but I requested the maker to give them; and they are sent accordingly.—The sooner it is put up the better; but be sure it is done, the wood part (of what is sent) must receive a coat of white paint.—The spire (if it is not the case already) must have that of black; the bill of the bird is to be black,—and the olive branch in the mouth of it must be green; these two last are otherwise by mistake.—Great pains (and Mr. Lear understands the Compass) must be taken to fix the points truly; otherwise they will deceive rather than direct—(if they vary from the North, South, East, and West).

*The weather vane that General Washington selected and sent down from Philadelphia while attending the Constitutional Convention in the summer of 1787 features a dove with an olive branch; the supporting shaft also serves as a lightning rod. It seems peculiarly fitting that this symbol of peace, which still adorns and protects Mount Vernon, should be contemporaneous with the Federal Constitution, to the creation of which George Washington contributed so indispensably in Philadelphia that same summer.*

# INDEX

*Pages with illustrations appear in italics.*